Living Lessons
of
Life and Love

Living Lessons
of
Life and Love

Ruth, Esther, Job, Ecclesiastes and Song of Solomon

*Paraphrased
by Kenneth N. Taylor*

Preface

The Scriptures are not unaware of mankind's very human problems of love, depression, joy, and despair. Here in this little volume are some of the most fascinating portions of the entire Bible. They lay bare the soul of the godly, revealing all these emotions in abundance.

The book of *Ruth* tells about the grace of God in the life of a young Gentile woman—who became a direct ancestress of Jesus Christ the Messiah. Her persistence in love for her mother-in-law was richly rewarded in her own life as well as in all future generations.

The story of *Esther* is a wild one. She was a sensitive Jewess, though ruthless in the avenging of her people— a victim of the murderous times, a product of her environment. As a result of her beauty, refinement, courage, trust in God, and obedience to her elder cousin's advice, she saved millions of Jews from an ancient Buchenwald. This is history told like the most exciting fiction.

Ecclesiastes is a dirge of despair, the thoughts of a man who, despite his opportunities, knew all too little of God. And so, although he had immense wealth and power, he had little of joy.

Job is the story of personal Satanic powers at work to destroy a man's body and soul. Job's anguish in his darkness is terrible to see. God's vindication of Job's sporadic heights of trust is heartening to any modern under Satanic pressures.

The Song of Solomon is an esoteric love poem by a

man with 60 wives (eventually 700 of them, plus 300 concubines) who writes love lyrics to his latest find. However, this allegory has through the ages been thought by Jews to refer to God's love for Israel, and by Christians to be a symbolism of God's love for His Church.

Each of these Bible portions is part of the Book concerning which the Apostle Paul declared, "The whole Bible was given to us by inspiration from God and is useful to teach us what is true and to make us realize what is wrong in our lives; it straightens us out and helps us do what is right. It is God's way of making us well-prepared at every point, fully equipped to do good to everyone."*

So—take, read, and grow in godliness and power. This little volume is all part of God's Word to you.

*2 Timothy 3:16, 17, Living New Testament

From Wm. Tyndale's Prologue to the First Printed English New Testament:

Exhortynge instantly and besechynge those that are better sene in the tongues than I, and that have higher gifts of grace to interpret the sense of Scripture, and meaning of the Spirit, than I, to consider and ponder my labor, and that with the spirit of meekness. And if they perceive in any places that I have not attained the very sense of the tongue, or meaning of the Scripture, or have not given the right English word, that they put to their hands to amend it, remembering that so is their duty to do. For we have not received the gifts of God for ourselves only, or for to hide them; but for to bestow them unto the honoring of God and Christ and edifying of the congregation, which is the body of Christ.

CONTENTS

The Book of Ruth

CHAPTER 1

Long ago when judges ruled in Israel, a man named Elimelech, from Bethlehem,[1] left the country because of a famine and moved to the land of Moab. With him were his wife, Naomi, and his two sons, Mahlon and Chilion.

3 During the time of their residence there, Elimelech died and Naomi was left with her two sons.

4, 5 These young men, Mahlon and Chilion, married girls of Moab, Orpah and Ruth. But later, both men died, so that Naomi was left alone, without her husband or sons.

6, 7 She decided to return to Israel with her daughters-in-law, for she had heard that the Lord had blessed His people by giving them good crops again.

8 But after they had begun their homeward journey, she changed her mind and said to her two daughters-in-law, "Why don't you return to your parents' homes instead of coming with me? And may the Lord reward you for your faithfulness to your husbands and to me.

9 And may He bless you with another happy mar-

---

[1]Literally, "They were Ephrathites from Bethlehem in Judah."

riage." Then she kissed them and they all broke down and cried.

10 "No," they said. "We want to go with you to your people."

11 But Naomi replied, "It is better for you to return to your own people. Do I have younger sons who could grow up to be your husbands?[2]

12 No, my daughters, return to your parents' homes, for I am too old to have a husband. And even if that were possible, and I became pregnant tonight, and bore sons,

13 Would you wait for them to grow up? No, of course not, my daughters; oh, how I grieve for you that the Lord has punished me in a way that injures you."

14 And again they cried together, and Orpah kissed her mother-in-law good-bye, and returned to her childhood home; but Ruth insisted on staying with Naomi.

15 "See," Naomi said to her, "your sister-in-law has gone back to her people and to her gods; you should do the same."

16 But Ruth replied, "Don't make me leave you, for I want to go wherever you go, and to live wherever you live; your people shall be my people, and your God shall be my God;

17 I want to die where you die, and be buried there. May the Lord do terrible things to me if I allow anything but death to separate us."

18 And when Naomi saw that Ruth had made up

---

[2]This refers to the custom of the day. Parents kept a widowed daughter-in-law in the family by marrying her off to a younger brother of her former husband. See Deuteronomy 25:5-10.

her mind and could not be persuaded otherwise, she stopped urging her.

19   So they both came to Bethlehem and the entire village was stirred by their arrival. "Is it really Naomi?" the women asked.

20   But she told them, "Don't call me Naomi. Call me Mara," (Naomi means "pleasant"; Mara means "bitter") "for Almighty God has dealt me bitter blows.

21   I went out full and the Lord has brought me home empty; why should you call me Naomi when the Lord has turned His back on me and sent such calamity!"

22   (Their return from Moab and arrival in Bethlehem was at the beginning of the barley harvest.)

CHAPTER 2

Now Naomi had an in-law there in Bethlehem who was a very wealthy man. His name was Boaz.

2   One day Ruth said to Naomi, "Perhaps I can go out into the fields of some kind man to glean the free grain[1] behind his reapers." And Naomi said, "All right, dear daughter. Go ahead."

3   So she did. And as it happened, the field where she found herself belonged to Boaz, this relative of Naomi's husband.

4, 5   Boaz arrived from the city while she was there. After exchanging greetings with the reapers he said to his foreman, "Hey, who's that girl over there?"

---

[1]See Leviticus 19:9 and Deuteronomy 24:19.

6 And the foreman replied, "It's that girl from the land of Moab who came back with Naomi.

7 She asked me this morning if she could pick up the grains dropped by the reapers, and she has been at it ever since except for a few minutes' rest over there in the shade."

8, 9 Boaz went over and talked to her, "Listen, my child," he said to her. "Stay right here with us to glean; don't think of going to any other fields. Stay right behind my women workers; I have warned the young men not to bother you; when you are thirsty, go and help yourself to the water."

10, 11 She thanked him warmly. "How can you be so kind to me?" she asked. "You must know I am only a foreigner."

"Yes, I know," Boaz replied, "and I also know about all the love and kindness you have shown your mother-in-law since the death of your husband, and how you left your father and mother in your own land and have come here to live among strangers.

12 May the Lord God of Israel, under whose wings you have come to take refuge, bless you for it."

13 "Oh, thank you, sir," she replied, "You are so good to me, and I'm not even one of your workers!"

14 At lunch time Boaz called to her, "Come and eat with us." So she sat with his reapers and he gave her food,[2] more than she could eat.

15 And when she went back to work again, Boaz told his young men to let her glean right among the sheaves without stopping her,

---

[2]Literally, "ate the parched grain and dipped her morsels of food in the wine."

16   And to snap off some heads of barley and drop them on purpose for her to glean, and not to make any remarks.

17   So she worked there all day, and in the evening when she had beaten out the barley she had gleaned, it came to a whole bushel!

18   She carried it back into the city and gave it to her mother-in-law, with what was left of her lunch.

19   "So much!" Naomi exclaimed. "Where in the world did you glean today? Praise the Lord for whoever was so kind to you." So Ruth told her mother-in-law all about it, and mentioned that the owner of the field was Boaz.

20   "Praise the Lord for a man like that! God has continued His kindness to us as well as to your dead husband!" Naomi cried excitedly—"Why, that man is one of our closest relatives[3]!"

21   "Well," Ruth told her, "he said to come back and stay close behind his reapers until the entire field is harvested."

22   "This is wonderful!" Naomi exclaimed. "Do as he has said. Stay with his girls right through the whole harvest; you will be safer there than in any other field!"

23   So Ruth did, and gleaned with them until the end of the barley harvest, and then the wheat harvest, too.

---

[3]Literally, "a near relative, one of our redeemers."

CHAPTER 3

One day Naomi said to Ruth, "My dear, isn't it time that I try to find a husband for you, and get you happily married again?

2 The man I'm thinking of is Boaz! He has been so kind to us, and is a close relative. I happen to know that he will be winnowing barley tonight out on the threshing-floor.

3 Now do what I tell you—bathe and put on some perfume and some nice clothes and go on down to the threshing-floor, but don't let him see you until he has finished his supper.

4 Notice where he lies down to sleep; then go and lift the cover off his feet and lie down there, and he will tell you what to do concerning marriage."

5 And Ruth replied, "All right. I'll do whatever you say."

6, 7 So she went down to the threshing-floor that night and followed her mother-in-law's instructions. After Boaz had finished a good meal, he lay down very contentedly beside a heap of grain and went to sleep. Then Ruth came quietly and lifted the covering off his feet and lay there.

8 Suddenly, around midnight, he wakened and sat up, startled. There was a woman lying at his feet!

9 "Who are you?" he demanded.

"It's I, sir—Ruth," she replied. "Make me your wife according to God's law, for you are my close relative."

10 "Thank God for a girl like you!" he exclaimed. "For you are being even kinder to Naomi now than

before. Naturally you'd prefer a younger man, even though poor. But you have put aside your personal desires [so that you can give Naomi an heir by marrying me.[1]]

11   Now don't worry about a thing, my child; I'll handle all the details, for everyone knows what a wonderful person you are.

12   But there is one problem. It's true that I am a close relative, but there is someone else who is more closely related to you than I am.

13   Stay here tonight, and in the morning I'll talk to him, and if he will marry you, fine; let him do his duty; but if he won't, then I will, I swear by Jehovah; lie down until the morning."

14   So she lay at his feet until the morning and was up early, before daybreak, for he had said to her, "Don't let it be known that a woman was here at the threshing-floor."

15-18   "Bring your shawl," he told her. She opened it up and he poured in a bushel and a half of barley as a present for her mother-in-law.

"Well, what happened, dear?" Naomi asked her when she arrived home. She told Naomi everything and gave her the barley from Boaz, and mentioned his remark that she mustn't go home without a present. Then Naomi said to her, "Just be patient until we hear what happens, for Boaz won't rest until he has followed through on this. He'll settle it today."

---

[1] Implied.

CHAPTER 4

So Boaz went down to the market place[1] and found the relative he had mentioned. "Say, come over here," he called to him. "I want to talk to you a minute." So they sat down together.

2   Then Boaz called for ten of the chief men of the village, and asked them to sit as witnesses.

3   Boaz said to his relative, "You know Naomi, who came back to us from Moab. She is selling our brother Elimelech's property.

4   I felt that I should speak to you about it so that you can buy it if you wish, with these respected men as witnesses. If you want it,[2] let me know right away, for if you don't take it, I will. You have the first right to purchase it and I am next."

The man replied, "All right, I'll buy it."

5   Then Boaz told him, "Your purchase of the land from Naomi requires your marriage to Ruth so that she can have children to carry on her husband's name, and to inherit the land."

6   "Then I can't do it," the man replied. "For her son would become an heir to my property, too;[3] you buy it."

7   In those days it was the custom in Israel for a man transferring a right of purchase to pull off his

---

[1]Literally, "the gate" of the city, where legal affairs were usually transacted.
[2]Literally, "if you want to redeem it."
[3]Or, "that would ruin my own inheritance," i.e., complicate his estate for the children he already had.

sandal and hand it to the other party; this publicly validated the transaction.

8 So, as the man said to Boaz, "You buy it for yourself," he drew off his sandal.

9 Then Boaz said to the witnesses and to the crowd standing around, "You have seen that today I have bought all the property of Elimelech, Chilion, and Mahlon, from Naomi,

10 And that with it I have purchased Ruth the Moabitess, the widow of Mahlon, to be my wife, so that she can have a son to carry on the family name of her dead husband."

11 And all the people standing there, and the witnesses replied, "We are witnesses. May the Lord make this woman, who has now come into your home, as fertile as Rachel and Leah, from whom all the nation of Israel descended! May you be a great and successful man in Bethlehem,

12 And may the descendants the Lord will give you from this young woman be as numerous and honorable as those of our ancestor Perez, the son of Tamar and Judah."

13 So Boaz married Ruth, and when he slept with her, the Lord gave her a son.

14 And the women of the city said to Naomi, "Bless the Lord who has given you this little grandson; may he be famous in Israel.

15 May he restore your youth and take care of you in your old age; for he is the son of your daughter-in-law who loves you so much, and who has been kinder to you than seven sons!"

16, 17   Naomi took care of the baby, and the neighbor women said, "Now at last Naomi has a son again!"

And they named him Obed. He was the father of Jesse and grandfather of King David.

18   This is the family tree of Boaz, beginning with his ancestor Perez:

19   Perez
      Hezron
      Ram
      Amminadab

20   Nashon
      Salmon

21   Boaz
      Obed

22   Jesse
      David

Esther

CHAPTER 1

It was the third year of the reign of King Ahasuerus, emperor of vast Media-Persia, with its 127 provinces stretching from India to Ethiopia. This was the year of the great celebration at Shushan Palace, to which the emperor invited all his governors, aides, and army officers, bringing them in from every part of Media-Persia for the occasion.

4 The celebration lasted six months, a tremendous display of the wealth and glory of his empire.

5 When it was all over, the king gave a special party for the palace servants and officials—janitors and cabinet officials alike—for seven days of revelry, held in the courtyard of the palace garden.

6 The decorations were green, white, and blue, fastened with purple ribbons[1] tied to silver rings imbedded in marble pillars! Gold and silver benches stood on pavements of black, red, white, and yellow marble!

7 Drinks were served in golden goblets of many designs, and there was an abundance of royal wine, for the king was feeling very generous.

---

[1]Literally, "fastened with cords of fine linen and purple thread."

8   The only restriction on the drinking was that no one should be compelled to take more than he wanted, but those who wished could have as much as they pleased. For the king had instructed his officers to let everyone decide this matter for himself!

9   Queen Vashti gave a party for the women of the palace at the same time.

10   On the final day, when the king was feeling high, half-drunk from wine, he told the seven eunuchs who were his personal aides—Mehuman, Biztha, Harbona, Bigtha, Abagtha, Zethar, and Carkas—

11   To bring Queen Vashti to him with the royal crown upon her head so that all the men could gaze upon her beauty—for she was a very beautiful woman.

12   But when they conveyed the emperor's order to Queen Vashti, she refused to come. The king was furious,

13-15   But first consulted his lawyers, for he did nothing without their advice. They were men of wisdom who knew the temper of the times as well as Persian law and justice, and the king trusted their judgment. These men were Carshena, Shethar, Admatha, Tarshish, Meres, Marsena, and Memucan—seven high officials of Media-Persia. They were his personal friends as well as being the chief officers of the government.

"What shall we do about this situation?" he asked them. "What penalty does the law provide for a queen who refuses to obey the king's orders, properly sent through his aides?"

16   Memucan answered for the others, "Queen Vashti has wronged not only the king but every official and citizen of your empire.

17   For women everywhere will begin to disobey their husbands when they learn what Queen Vashti has done.

18   And before this day is out, the wife of every one of us officials throughout your empire will hear what the queen did and will start talking to us husbands the same way, and there will be contempt and anger throughout your realm.

19   We suggest that, subject to your agreement, you issue a royal edict, a law of the Medes and Persians that can never be changed, that Queen Vashti be forever banished from your presence and that you choose another queen more worthy than she.

20   When this decree is published throughout your great kingdom, husbands everywhere, whatever their rank, will be respected by their wives!"

21   The king and all his aides thought this made good sense, so he followed Memucan's counsel.

22   And sent letters to all of his provinces, in all the local languages, stressing that every man should rule his home, and should assert his authority.

CHAPTER 2

But after King Ahasuerus' anger had cooled, he began brooding over the loss of Vashti, realizing that he would never see her again.

2   So his aides suggested, "Let us go and find the most beautiful girls in the empire and bring them to the king for his pleasure.

3   We will appoint agents in each province to select

young lovelies for the royal harem. Hegai, the eunuch in charge, will see that they are given beauty treatments,

4 And after that, the girl who pleases you most shall be the queen instead of Vashti." This suggestion naturally pleased the king very much, and he put the plan into immediate effect.

5 Now there was a certain Jew at the palace named Mordecai (son of Jair, son of Shimei, son of Kish, a Benjaminite).

6 He had been captured when Jerusalem was destroyed by King Nebuchadnezzar, and had been exiled to Babylon along with King Jeconiah of Judah and many others.

7 This man had a beautiful and lovely young cousin[1], Hadassah (also called Esther), whose father and mother were dead, and whom he had adopted into his family and raised as his own daughter.

8 So now, as a result of the king's decree, Esther was brought to the king's harem at Shushan Palace, along with many other young girls.

9 Hegai, who was responsible for the harem, was very much impressed with her, and did his best to make her happy; he ordered a special menu for her, favored her for the beauty treatments, gave her seven girls from the palace as her maids, and gave her the most luxurious apartment in the harem.

10 Esther hadn't told anyone that she was a Jewess, for Mordecai had said not to.

11 He came daily to the court of the harem to ask about Esther and to find out what was happening to her.

---

[1] His uncle's daughter.

12-14   The instructions concerning these girls were that before being taken to the king's bed, each would be given six months of beauty treatments with oil of myrrh, followed by six months with special perfumes and ointments. Then, as each girl's turn came for spending the night with King Ahasuerus, she was given her choice of clothing or jewelry she wished, to enhance her beauty. She was taken to the king's apartment in the evening and the next morning returned to the second harem where the king's wives lived. There she was under the care of Shaashgaz, another of the king's eunuchs, and lived there the rest of her life, never seeing the king again unless he had especially enjoyed her, and called for her by name.

15   When it was Esther's[2] turn to go to the king, she accepted the advice of Hegai, the eunuch in charge of the harem, dressing according to his instructions. And all the other girls exclaimed with delight when they saw her.

16   So Esther was taken to the palace of the king in January of the seventh year of his reign.

17   Well, the king loved Esther more than any of the other girls. He was so delighted with her that he set the royal crown on her head and declared her queen instead of Vashti.

18   To celebrate the occasion, he threw another big party for all his officials and servants, giving generous gifts to everyone and making grants to the provinces in the form of remission of taxes.

19   [Later, the king demanded a second bevy of

---

[2]Literally, "Esther, the daughter of Abihail who was Mordecai's uncle, who had adopted her."

beautiful girls;³ by that time Mordecai had become a government official.)

20   Esther still hadn't told anyone she was a Jewess, for she was still following Mordecai's orders, just as she had in his home.

21   One day, as Mordecai was on duty at the palace, two of the king's eunuchs, Bigthan and Teresh—who were guards at the palace gate—became angry at the king and plotted to assassinate him.

22   Mordecai heard about it and passed on the information to Queen Esther, who told the king, crediting Mordecai with the information.

23   An inquisition was held, the two men found guilty, and impaled alive.⁴ This was all duly recorded in the book of the history of King Ahasuerus' reign.

CHAPTER 3

Soon afterwards King Ahasuerus appointed Haman (son of Hammedatha the Agagite), as prime minister. He was the most powerful official in the empire next to the king himself.

2   Now all the king's officials bowed before him in deep reverence whenever he passed by, for so the king had commanded. But Mordecai refused to bow.

3, 4   "Why are you disobeying the king's commandment?" the others demanded day after day, but he still refused. Finally they spoke to Haman about it, to see

---

³Or, "When Esther and the other girls had been transferred to the second harem."
⁴Literally, "hanged on a tree." Possibly the meaning is that they were crucified.

whether Mordecai could get away with it because of his being a Jew, which was the excuse he had given them.

6   Haman decided, however, not to lay hands on Mordecai alone, but to move against all of Mordecai's people, the Jews, and destroy all of them throughout the whole kingdom of Ahasuerus.

7   The most propitious time for this action was determined by throwing dice. This was done in April of the 12th year of the reign of Ahasuerus, and February of the following year was the date indicated.

8   Haman now approached the king about the matter. "There is a certain race of people scattered through all the provinces of your kingdom," he began, "and their laws are different from those of any other nation, and they refuse to obey the king's laws; therefore, it is not in the king's interest to let them live.

9   If it please the king, issue a decree that they be destroyed, and I will pay $20,000,000 into the royal treasury for the expenses involved in this purge."

10   The king agreed, confirming his decision by removing his ring from his finger and giving it to Haman[1], telling him,

11   "Keep the money, but go ahead and do as you like with these people—whatever you think best."

12   Two or three weeks later,[2] Haman called in the king's secretaries and dictated letters to the governors and officials throughout the empire, to each province in its own languages and dialects; these letters were signed in the name of King Ahasuerus and sealed with his ring.

---

[1]Literally, "Haman, son of Hammedatha the Agagite."
[2]Literally, "Then, on the 13th day of the first month . . ."

13   They were then sent by messengers into all the provinces of the empire, decreeing that the Jews—young and old, women and children—must all be killed on the 13th day of February of the following year, and their property given to those who killed them.

14   "A copy of this edict," the letter stated, "must be proclaimed as law in every province, and made known to all your people, so that they will be ready to do their duty on the appointed day."

15   The edict went out by the king's speediest couriers, after being first proclaimed in the city of Shushan. Then the king and Haman sat down for a drinking spree as the city fell into confusion and panic.

CHAPTER 4

When Mordecai learned what had been done, he tore his clothes and put on sackcloth and ashes, and went out into the city, crying with a loud and bitter wail.

2   Then he stood outside the gate of the palace, for no one was permitted to enter in mourning clothes.

3   And throughout all the provinces there was great mourning among the Jews, fasting, weeping, and despair at the king's decree; and many lay in sackcloth and ashes.

4   When Esther's maids and eunuchs came and told her about Mordecai, she was deeply distressed and sent clothing to him to replace the sackcloth, but he refused it.

5   Then Esther sent for Hathach, one of the king's eunuchs who had been appointed as her attendant, and

told him to go out to Mordecai and find out what the trouble was, and why he was acting like that.

6 So Hathach went out to the city square, and found Mordecai just outside the palace gates,

7 And heard the whole story from him; and about the $20,000,000 Haman had promised to pay into the king's treasury for the destruction of the Jews.

8 Mordecai also gave Hathach a copy of the king's decree dooming all Jews, and told him to show it to Esther and to tell her what was happening, and that she should go to the king to plead for her people.

9 So Hathach returned to Esther with Mordecai's message.

10 Esther told Hathach to go back and say to Mordecai,

11 "All the world knows that anyone, whether man or woman, who goes into the king's inner court without his summons is doomed to die unless the king holds out his golden scepter; and the king has not called for me to come to him in more than a month."

12 So Hathach gave Esther's message to Mordecai.

13 This was Mordecai's reply to Esther: "Do you think you will escape there in the palace, when all other Jews are killed?

14 If you keep quiet at a time like this, God will deliver the Jews from some other source, but you and your relatives will die; what's more, who can say but that God has brought you into the palace for just such a time as this?"

15 Then Esther said to tell Mordecai:

16 "Go and gather together all the Jews of Shushan

and fast for me; do not eat or drink for three days, night or day; and I and my maids will do the same; and then, though it is strictly forbidden, I will go in to see the king; and if I perish, I perish."

17 So Mordecai did as Esther told him to.

CHAPTER 5

Three days later Esther put on her royal robes and entered the inner court just beyond the royal hall of the palace, where the king was sitting upon his royal throne.

2 And when he saw Queen Esther standing there in the inner court, he welcomed her, holding out the golden scepter to her. So Esther approached and touched its tip.

3 Then the king asked her, "What do you wish, Queen Esther? What is your request? I will give it to you, even if it is half the kingdom!"

4 And Esther replied, "If it please Your Majesty, I want you and Haman to come to a banquet I have prepared for you today."

5 The king turned to his aides. "Tell Haman to hurry!" he said. So the king and Haman came to Esther's banquet.

6 During the wine course the king said to Esther, "Now tell me what you really want, and I will give it to you, even if it is half of the kingdom!"

7, 8 Esther replied, "My request, my deepest wish, is that if Your Majesty loves me, and wants to grant my request, that you come again with Haman tomorrow to the banquet I shall prepare for you. And tomorrow I will explain what this is all about."

9   What a happy man was Haman as he left the banquet! But when he saw Mordecai there at the gate, not standing up or trembling before him, he was furious.

10   However, he restrained himself and went on home and gathered together his friends and Zeresh his wife,

11   And boasted to them about his wealth, and his many children, and promotions the king had given him, and how he had become the greatest man in the kingdom next to the king himself.

12   Then he delivered his final punch line: "Yes, and Esther the queen invited only me and the king himself to the banquet she prepared for us; and tomorrow we are invited again!

13   But yet," he added, "all this is nothing when I see Mordecai the Jew just sitting there in front of the king's gate, refusing to bow to me."

14   "Well," suggested Zeresh his wife and all his friends, "Get ready a 75-foot-high gallows, and in the morning ask the king to let you hang Mordecai on it; and when this is done you can go on your merry way with the king to the banquet." This pleased Haman immensely and he ordered the gallows built.

CHAPTER 6

That night the king had trouble sleeping and decided to read awhile. He ordered the historical records of his kingdom from the library, and in them he came across the item telling how Mordecai had exposed the plot of Bigthana and Teresh, two of the king's eunuchs, watchmen at the palace gates, who had plotted to assassinate him.

3 "What reward did we ever give Mordecai for this?" the king asked; and his courtiers replied, "Nothing!"

4 "Who is on duty in the outer court?" the king inquired. Now as it happened, Haman had just arrived in the outer court of the palace to ask the king to hang Mordecai from the gallows he was building.

5 So the courtiers replied to the king, "Haman is out there."

"Bring him in," the king ordered.

6 So Haman came in and the king said to him, "What should I do to honor a man who truly pleases me?"

Haman thought to himself, "Who would he want to honor more than me?"

7, 8 So he replied, "Bring out some of the royal robes the king himself has worn, and the king's own horse, and the royal crown,

9 And instruct one of the king's most noble princes to robe the man and to lead him through the streets on the king's own horse, shouting before him, 'This is the way the king honors those who truly please him!' "

10 "Excellent!" the king said to Haman. "Hurry and take these robes and my horse, and do just as you have said—to Mordecai the Jew, who works at the Chancellory. Follow every detail you have suggested."

11 So Haman took the robes and put them on

Mordecai and mounted him on the king's own steed, and led him through the streets of the city, shouting, "This is the way the king honors those he delights in."

12 Afterwards Mordecai returned to his job, but Haman hurried home utterly humiliated.

13 When Haman told Zeresh his wife and all his friends what had happened, they said, "If Mordecai is a Jew, you will never succeed in your plans against him; to continue to oppose him will be fatal."

14 While they were still discussing it with him, the king's messengers arrived to conduct Haman quickly to the banquet Esther had prepared.

CHAPTER 7

So the king and Haman came to Esther's banquet.

2 And again, during the wine course, the king asked her, "What is your petition, Queen Esther? What do you wish? Whatever it is, I will give it to you, even if it is half of my kingdom!"

3 And at last Queen Esther replied, "If I have won your favor, O king, and if it please Your Majesty, save my life and the lives of my people.

4 For I and my people have been sold to those who will destroy us. We are doomed to destruction and slaughter. If we were only to be sold as slaves, perhaps I could remain quiet, though even then there would be incalculable damage to the king that no amount of money could begin to cover."

5 "What are you talking about?" King Ahasuerus demanded. "Who would dare touch you?"

6　Esther replied, "This wicked Haman is our enemy." Then Haman grew pale with fright before the king and queen.

7　The king jumped to his feet and went out into the palace garden as Haman stood up to plead for his life to Queen Esther, for he knew that he was doomed.

8　In despair he fell upon the couch where Queen Esther was reclining, just as the king returned from the palace garden.

"Will he even rape the queen right here in the palace, before my very eyes?" the king roared. Instantly the death veil was placed over Haman's face.

9　Then Harbona, one of the king's aides, said, "Sir, Haman has just ordered a 75-foot gallows constructed, to hang Mordecai, the man who saved the king from assassination! It stands in Haman's courtyard."

"Hang Haman on it," the king ordered.

10　So they did, and the king's wrath was pacified.

CHAPTER 8

On that same day King Ahasuerus gave the estate of Haman, the Jew's enemy, to Queen Esther. Then Mordecai was brought before the king, for Esther had told the king that he was her cousin and step-father.[1]

2　The king took off his ring—which he had taken back from Haman—and gave it to Mordecai, [appointing him Prime Minister[2]]; and Esther appointed Mordecai to be in charge of Haman's estate.

---

[1] Literally, "had made known how they were related."
[2] Implied.

3   And now once more Esther came before the king, falling down at his feet and begging him with tears to stop Haman's plot against the Jews.

4   And again the king held out the golden scepter to Esther. So she arose and stood before him,

5   And said, "If it please Your Majesty, and if you love me, send out a decree reversing Haman's order to destroy the Jews throughout the king's provinces

6   For how can I endure it, to see my people butchered and destroyed?"

7   Then King Ahasuerus said to Queen Esther and Mordecai the Jew, "I have given Esther the palace of Haman and he has been hanged upon the gallows because he tried to destroy you.

8   Now go ahead and send a message to the Jews, telling them whatever you want to in the king's name, and seal it with the king's ring, so that it can never be reversed.[3]"

9, 10   Immediately the king's secretaries were called in—it was now the 23rd day of the month of July—and they wrote as Mordecai dictated—a decree to the Jews and to the officials, governors, and princes of all the provinces from India to Ethiopia, 127 in all; the decree was translated into the languages and dialects of all the people of the kingdom. Mordecai wrote in the name of King Ahasuerus and sealed the message with the king's ring and sent the letters by swift carriers—riders on

---

[3]Haman's message, too, had been sealed with the king's ring and could not be reversed, even by the king. This was part of the famed "law of the Medes and Persians." Now the king is giving permission for whatever other decree Mordecai can devise that will offset the first, without actually cancelling it.

camels, mules, and young dromedaries used in the king's service.

11 This decree gave the Jews everywhere permission to unite in the defense of their lives and their families, to destroy all the forces opposed to them, and to take their property.

12 The day chosen for this throughout all the provinces of King Ahasuerus was the 13th day of March![4]

13 It further stated that a copy of this decree, which must be recognized everywhere as law, must be broadcast to all the people so that the Jews would be ready and prepared to overcome their enemies.

14 So the mail went out swiftly, carried by the king's couriers and speeded by the king's commandment. The same decree was also issued at Shushan Palace.

15 Then Mordecai put on the royal robes of blue and white and the great crown of gold, with an outer cloak of fine linen and purple, and went out from the presence of the king through the city streets filled with shouting people.

16 And the Jews had joy and gladness, and were honored everywhere.

17 And in every city and province, as the king's decree arrived, the Jews were filled with joy and had a great celebration and declared a holiday. And many of the people of the land pretended to be Jews, for they feared what the Jews might do to them.

---

[4]This was the same day as was set by Haman for the extermination of the Jews.

CHAPTER 9

So on the 13th day of March, the day the two decrees of the king were to be put into effect—the day the Jews' enemies had hoped to vanquish them, though it turned out quite to the contrary—the Jews gathered in their cities throughout all the king's provinces to defend themselves against any who might try to harm them; but no one tried, for they were greatly feared.

3 And all the rulers of the provinces—the governors, officials, and aides—helped the Jews for fear of Mordecai;

4 For Mordecai was a mighty name in the king's palace and his fame was known throughout all the provinces; for he had become more and more powerful.

5 But the Jews went ahead on that appointed day and slaughtered their enemies.

6 They even killed 500 men in Shushan.

7-10 They also killed the ten sons of Haman (son of Hammedatha), the Jews' enemy—

       Parshandatha
       Dalphon
       Aspatha
       Poratha
       Adalia
       Aridatha
       Parmashta
       Arisai
       Aridai, and
       Vaizatha

But they did not try to take Haman's property.

11 Late that evening, when the king was informed of the number of those slain in Shushan,

12 He called for Queen Esther. "The Jews have killed 500 men in Shushan alone," he exclaimed, "and also Haman's ten sons. If they have done that here, I wonder what has happened in the rest of the provinces! But now, what more do you want? It will be granted to you. Tell me and I will do it."

13 And Esther said, "If it please Your Majesty, let the Jews who are here at Shushan do again tomorrow as they have done today, and let Haman's ten sons be hanged upon the gallows."

14 So the king agreed, and the decree was announced at Shushan, and they hung up the bodies of Haman's ten sons.

15 Then the Jews at Shushan gathered together the next day also and killed 300 more men, though again they took no property.

16 Meanwhile, the other Jews throughout the king's provinces had gathered together and stood for their lives and destroyed all their enemies, killing 75,000 of those who hated them; but they did not take their goods.

17 Throughout the provinces this was done on the 13th day of March, and the next day they rested, celebrating their victory with feasting and gladness.

18 But the Jews at Shushan went on killing their enemies the second day also, and rested the 15th day, with feasting and gladness.

19 And so it is that the Jews in the unwalled villages throughout Israel to this day have an annual celebration on the 14th day of the month, rejoicing and sending gifts to each other.

20 Mordecai wrote a history of all these events, and sent letters to the Jews near and far, throughout all the king's provinces,

21 Encouraging them to declare an annual holiday on the 14th and 15th of March,

22 To celebrate with feasting, gladness, and the giving of gifts this historic day when the Jews were saved from their enemies, when their sorrow was turned to gladness and their mourning into happiness.

23 So the Jews adopted Mordecai's suggestion and began this annual custom,

24, 25 As a reminder of the time when Haman (son of Hammedatha the Agagite), the enemy of all the Jews, had plotted to destroy them at the time determined by a throw of the dice; and to remind them that when the matter came before the king, he issued a decree causing Haman's plot to boomerang, and he and his sons were hanged on the gallows.

26 That is why this celebration is called "Purim," because the word for "throwing dice" in Persian is "pur."

27 All the Jews throughout the realm agreed to inaugurate this tradition and to pass it on to their descendants and to all who became Jews; they declared they would never fail to celebrate these two days at the appointed time each year.

28 It would be an annual event from generation to generation, celebrated by every family throughout the countryside and cities of the empire, so that the memory of what had happened would never perish from the Jewish race.

29 Meanwhile, Queen Esther (daughter of Abihail and later adopted by Mordecai the Jew) had written a letter throwing her full support behind Mordecai's letter inaugurating his annual feast of Purim.

In addition, letters were sent to all the Jews throughout the 127 provinces of the kingdom of Ahasuerus with messages of good will, and encouragement to confirm these two days annually as the Feast of Purim, decreed by both Mordecai the Jew and by Queen Esther; indeed, the Jews themselves had decided upon this tradition as a remembrance of the time of their national fasting and prayer.

32 So the commandment of Esther confirmed these dates and it was recorded as law.

CHAPTER 10

King Ahasuerus not only laid tribute upon the mainland, but even on the islands of the sea!

2 His great deeds, and also the full account of the greatness of Mordecai and the honors given him by the king, are written in The Book of the Chronicles of the Kings of Media and Persia.

3 For Mordecai the Jew was the Prime Minister, with authority next to that of King Ahasuerus himself. He was, of course, very great among the Jews, and respected by all his countrymen because he did his best for his people, and was a friend at court for all of them.

Ecclesiastes

CHAPTER 1

The author: Solomon[1] of Jerusalem, King David's son, "The Preacher."

2 In my opinion, nothing is worthwhile; everything is futile.

3-7 For what does a man get for all his hard work?

Generations come and go but it makes no difference.[2] The sun rises and sets and hurries around to rise again. The wind blows south and north, here and there, twisting back and forth, getting nowhere.[3] The rivers run into the sea but the sea is never full, and the water returns again to the rivers, and flows again to the sea . . .

8-11 Everything is unutterable weary and tiresome. No matter how much we see, we are never satisfied; no matter how much we hear, we are not content.

*   *   *   *   *

History merely repeats itself. Nothing is truly new; it has all been done or said before. What can you point to that is new? How do you know it didn't exist long ages ago? We don't remember what happened in

---

[1]Implied. Literally, "the words of the Preacher, the son (or descendant) of David, King in Jerusalem."
[2]Literally, "But the earth remains forever."
[3]Implied.

those former times, and in the future generations no one will remember what we have done back here.

*　　*　　*　　*　　*

12-15　I, the Preacher, was king of Israel, living in Jerusalem. And I applied myself to search for understanding about everything in the universe. I discovered that the lot of man, which God has dealt to him, is not a happy one. It is all foolishness, chasing the wind. What is wrong cannot be righted; it is water over the dam; and there is no use thinking of what might have been.

16-18　I said to myself, "Look, I am better educated than any of the kings before me in Jerusalem. I have greater wisdom and knowledge." So I worked hard to be wise instead of foolish[4]—but now I realize that even this was like chasing the wind. For the more my wisdom, the more my grief; to increase knowledge only increases distress.

CHAPTER 2

I said to myself, "Come now, be merry; enjoy yourself to the full." But I found that this, too, was futile. For it is silly to be laughing all the time; what good does it do?

*　　*　　*　　*　　*

3　So, after a lot of thinking, I decided to try the road of drink, while still holding steadily to my course of seeking wisdom.

Next I changed my course again and followed

---

[4] Or, "I sought to learn about composure and madness."

the path of folly, so that I could experience the only happiness most men have throughout their lives.

*   *   *   *   *

4, 5, 6   Then I tried to find fulfillment by inaugurating a great public works program: homes, vineyards, gardens, parks and orchards for myself, and reservoirs to hold the water to irrigate my plantations.

*   *   *   *   *

7, 8   Next I bought slaves, both men and women, and others were born within my household. I also bred great herds and flocks, more than any of the kings before me.

I collected silver and gold as taxes from many kings and provinces.

*   *   *   *   *

In the cultural arts, I organized men's and women's choirs and orchestras.

And then there were my many beautiful concubines.

*   *   *   *   *

9   So I became greater than any of the kings in Jerusalem before me, and with it all I remained clear-eyed, so that I could evaluate all these things.

10   Anything I wanted, I took, and did not restrain myself from any joy. I even found great pleasure in hard work. This pleasure was, indeed, my only reward for all my labors.

*   *   *   *   *

11   But as I looked at everything I had tried, it was all so useless, a chasing of the wind, and there was nothing really worthwhile anywhere.

12 Now I began a study of the comparative virtues of wisdom and folly, and anyone else would come to the same conclusion[1] I did—

13, 14 That wisdom is of more value than foolishness, just as light is better than darkness; for the wise man sees, while the fool is blind. And yet I noticed that there was one thing that happened to wise and foolish alike—

15. Just as the fool will die, so will I. So of what value is all my wisdom? Then I realized that even wisdom is futile.

16 For the wise and fool both die, and in the days to come both will be long forgotten.

17 So now I hate life because if is all so irrational; all is foolishness, chasing the wind.

* * * * *

18 And I am disgusted about this, that I must leave the fruits of all my hard work to others.

19 And who can tell whether my son will be a wise man or a fool? And yet all I have will be given to him—how discouraging!

20-23 So I turned in despair from hard work as the answer to my search for satisfaction. For though I spend my life searching for wisdom, knowledge, and skill, I must leave all of it to someone who hasn't done a day's work in his life; he inherits all my efforts, free of charge. This is not only foolish, but unfair. So what does a man get for all his hard work? Days full of sorrow and grief, and restless, bitter nights. It is all utterly ridiculous.

* * * * *

---

[1]Literally, "for what can the man do who comes after the king?"

24-26 So I decided that there was nothing better for a man to do than to enjoy his food and drink, and his job. Then I realized that even this pleasure is from the hand of God. For who can eat or enjoy apart from Him? For God gives those who please Him wisdom, knowledge, and joy; but if a sinner becomes wealthy, God takes the wealth away from him and gives it to those who please Him. So here, too, we see an example of foolishly chasing the wind.

CHAPTER 3

There is a right time for everything:

2 A time to be born;
A time to die;

A time to plant;
A time to harvest;

3 A time to kill;
A time to heal;

A time to destroy;
A time to rebuild;

4 A time to cry;
A time to laugh;

A time to grieve;
A time to dance;

5 A time for scattering stones;
A time for gathering stones;

A time to hug;
A time not to hug;

6 A time to find;
A time to lose;

A time for keeping;
A time for throwing away;

7 A time to tear;
A time to repair;

A time to be quiet;
A time to speak up;

8 A time for loving;
A time for hating;

A time for war;
A time for peace.

*   *   *   *   *

9 What does one really get from hard work?

10 I have thought about this in connection with all the various kinds of work God has given to mankind.

11 Everything is appropriate in its own time. But though God has planted eternity in the hearts of men, even so, man cannot see the whole scope of God's work from beginning to end.

12 So I conclude that, first, there is nothing better for a man than to be happy and to enjoy himself as long as he can;

13   And second, that he should eat and drink and enjoy the fruits of his labors, for these are gifts from God.

*   *   *   *   *

14   And I know this, that whatever God does is final—nothing can be added or taken from it; God's purpose in this is that man should fear the all-powerful God.[1]

*   *   *   *   *

15   Whatever is, has been long ago; and whatever is going to be has been before; God brings to pass again what was in the distant past and disappeared.[2]

16   Moreover, I notice that throughout the earth justice is giving way to crime and even the police courts are corrupt.

17   I said to myself, "In due season God will judge everything man does, both good and bad."

18   And then I realized that God is letting the world go on its sinful way so that He can test mankind, and so that men themselves will see that they are no better than beasts."

19   For men and animals both breathe the same air, and both die. So mankind has no real advantage over the beasts; what an absurdity!

20   All go to one place—the dust from which they came and to which they must return.

21   For who can prove that the spirit of man goes upward and the spirit of animals goes downward into dust?

22   So I saw that there is nothing better for men

---

[1]Implied.
[2]Literally, "God seeks what has been driven away."

than that they should be happy in their work, for that is what they are here for, and no one can bring them back to life to enjoy what will be in the future, so let them enjoy it now.

CHAPTER 4

Next I observed all the oppression and sadness throughout the earth—the tears of the oppressed, and no one helping them, while on the side of their oppressors were powerful allies.

2   So I felt that the dead were better off than the living.

3   And most fortunate of all are those who have never been born, and have never seen all the evil and crime throughout the earth.

4   Then I observed that the basic motive for success is the driving force of envy and jealousy! But this, too, is foolishness, chasing the wind.

5, 6   The fool won't work and almost starves, but feels that it is better to be lazy and barely get by, than to work hard when, in the long run, it is all so futile.

*   *   *   *   *

7   I also observed another piece of foolishness around the earth.

8   This is the case of a man who is quite alone, without a son or brother, yet he works hard to keep gaining more and more riches, and to whom will he leave it all? And why is he giving up so much now? It is all so pointless and depressing.

9   Two can accomplish more than twice as much as one, for the results can be much better.

10   If one falls, the other pulls him up; but if a man falls when he is alone, he's in trouble.

11   Also, on a cold night, two under the same blanket gain warmth from each other, but how can one be warm alone?

12   And one standing alone can be attacked and defeated, but two can stand back-to-back and conquer; three is even better, for a triple-braided cord is not easily broken.

*   *   *   *   *

13   It is better to be a poor but wise youth than to be an old and foolish king who refuses all advice.

14   Such a lad could come from prison and succeed. He might even become king, though born in poverty.

15   Everyone is eager to help a youth like that, even to help him usurp the throne.

16   He can become the leader of millions of people, and be very popular. But, then, the younger generation grows up around him and rejects him! So again, it is all foolishness, chasing the wind.

Chapter 5

As you enter the Temple, keep your ears open and your mouth shut! Don't be a fool who doesn't even realize it is sinful to make rash promises to God, for He is in heaven and you are only here on earth, so let your words be few. Just as being too busy gives you nightmares, so being a fool makes you a blabbermouth.

4 So when you talk to God and vow to Him that you will do something, don't delay in doing it, for God has no pleasure in fools. Keep your promise to Him.

5 It is far better not to say you'll do something than to say you will and then not do it.

6, 7 In that case, your mouth is making you sin. Don't try to defend yourself by telling the messenger from God that it was all a mistake [to make the vow[1]]. That would make God very angry; and He might[1] destroy your prosperity. Dreaming instead of doing is foolishness, and there is ruin in a flood of empty words; fear God instead.

*   *   *   *   *

8 If you see some poor man being oppressed by the rich, with miscarriage of justice anywhere throughout the land, don't be surprised! For every official is under orders from higher up, and the higher officials look up to their superiors! And so the matter is lost in red tape and bureaucracy.[2]

9 And over them all is the king. Oh, for a king who is devoted to his country! Only he can bring order from this chaos.

*   *   *   *   *

10 He who loves money shall never have enough. The foolishness of thinking that wealth brings happiness!

11 The more you have, the more you spend, right up to the limits of your income, so what is the advantage of wealth—except perhaps to watch it as it runs through your fingers!

---

[1]Implied.
[2]Literally, "and there are yet higher ones over them."

12   The man who works hard sleeps well whether he eats little or much, but the rich must worry and suffer insomnia.

*   *   *   *   *

13, 14   There is another serious problem I have seen everywhere—savings are put into risky investments that turn sour, and soon there is nothing left to pass on to one's son.

15   The man who speculates is soon back to where he began—with nothing.

16   This, as I said, is a very serious problem, for all his hard work has been for nothing; he has been working for the wind. It is all swept away.

17   All the rest of his life he is under a cloud—gloomy, discouraged, frustrated, and angry.

*   *   *   *   *

18   Well, one thing, at least, is good: it is for a man to eat well, drink a good glass of wine, accept his position in life, and enjoy his work whatever his job may be, for however long the Lord may let him live.

19, 20   And, of course, it is very good if a man has received wealth from the Lord, and the good health to enjoy it. To enjoy your work and to accept your lot in life—that is indeed a gift from God. The person who does that will not need to look back with sorrow on his past, for God gives him joy.

CHAPTER 6

Yes, but there is a very serious evil which I have seen everywhere—

2   God has given to some men very great wealth and honor, so that they can have everything they want, but He doesn't give them the health to enjoy it, and they die and others get it all! This is absurd, a hollow mockery, and a serious fault.

3   Even if a man has a hundred sons and as many daughters and lives to be very old, but leaves so little money at his death that his children can't even give him a decent burial—I say that he would be better off born dead.

4   For though his birth would then be futile and end in darkness, without even a name,

5   Never seeing the sun or even knowing its existence, yet that is better than to be an old, unhappy man.

6   Though a man lives a thousand years twice over, but doesn't find contentment—well, what's the use?

*   *   *   *   *

7, 8   Wise men and fools alike spend their lives scratching for food, and never seem to get enough. Both have the same problem, yet the poor man who is wise lives a far better life.

9   A bird in the hand is worth two in the bush: mere dreaming of nice things is foolish; it's chasing the wind.

*   *   *   *   *

10   All things are decided by fate; it was known long ago what each man would be. So there's no use arguing with God about your destiny.

11   The more words you speak, the less they mean, so why bother to speak at all?

12   In these few days of our empty lifetimes, who can say how one's days can best be spent? Who can

know what will prove best for the future after he is gone? For who knows the future?

CHAPTER 7

A good reputation is more valuable than the most expensive perfume.

*   *   *   *   *

The day one dies is better than the day he is born!

2 It is better to spend your time at funerals than at festivals. For you are going to die and it is a good thing to think about it while there is still time.

3 Sorrow is better than laughter, for sadness has a refining influence on us.

4 Yes, a wise man thinks much of death, while the fool thinks only of having a good time now.

*   *   *   *   *

5 It is better to be criticized by a wise man than to be praised by a fool!

6 For a fool's compliment is as quickly gone as paper in fire, and it is silly to be impressed by it.

*   *   *   *   *

7 The wise man is turned into a fool by a bribe; it destroys his understanding.

*   *   *   *   *

8 Finishing is better than starting!
Patience is better than pride!

9 Don't be quick-tempered—that is being a fool.

10 Don't long for "the good old days," for you don't know whether they were any better than these!

11 To be wise is as good as being rich; in fact, it is better.

12 You can get anything by either wisdom or money, but being wise has many advantages.

13 See the way God does things and fall into line. Don't fight the facts of nature.

14 Enjoy prosperity whenever you can, and when hard times strike, realize that God gives one as well as the other—so that everyone will realize that nothing is certain in this life.

* * * * *

15-17 In this silly life I have seen everything, including the fact that some of the good die young and some of the wicked live on and on. So don't be too good or too wise! Why destroy yourself? On the other hand, don't be too wicked either—don't be a fool! Why should you die before your time?

* * * * *

18 Tackle every task that comes along, and if you fear God you can expect His blessing.

19 A wise man is stronger than the mayors of ten big cities!

20 And there is not a single man in all the earth who is always good and never sins.

21, 22 Don't eavesdrop! You may hear your servant cursing you! For you know how often you yourself curse others!

* * * * *

23 I have tried my best to be wise. I declared, "I *will* be wise," but it didn't work.

24 Wisdom is far away, and very difficult to find.

25 I searched everywhere, determined to find wisdom and the reason for things, and to prove to myself the wickedness of folly, and that foolishness is madness.

* * * * *

26 A prostitute is more bitter than death.[1] May it please God that you escape from her, but sinners don't evade her snares.

* * * * *

27, 28 This is my conclusion, says the Preacher. Step by step I came to this result after researching in every direction: One tenth of one per cent of the men I interviewed could be said to be wise, but not one woman!

29 And I found that though God has made men upright, each has turned away to follow his own downward road.

CHAPTER 8

How wonderful to be wise, to understand things, to be able to analyze them and interpret them. Wisdom lights up a man's face, softening its hardness.

* * * * *

2, 3 Obey the king as you have vowed to do. Don't always be trying to get out of doing your duty, even when it's unpleasant. For the king punishes those who disobey.

---

[1] Literally, "the woman whose heart is snares and nets."

4 The king's command is backed by great power, and no one can withstand it or question it.

5 Those who obey him will not be punished. The wise man will find a time and a way to do what he says.

6, 7 Yes, there is a time and a way for everything, though man's trouble lies heavy upon him; for how can he avoid what he doesn't know is going to happen?

* * * * *

8 No one can hold back his spirit from departing; no one has the power to prevent his day of death, for there is no discharge from that obligation and that dark battle. Certainly a man's wickedness is not going to help him then.

* * * * *

9, 10 I have thought deeply about all that goes on here in the world, where people have the power of injuring each other. I have seen wicked men buried and as their friends returned from the cemetery, having forgotten all the dead man's evil deeds, these men were praised in the very city where they had committed their many crimes! How odd!

11 Because God does not punish sinners instantly, people feel it is safe to do wrong.

12 But though a man sins a hundred times and still lives, I know very well that those who fear God will be better off,

13 Unlike the wicked, who will not live long, good lives—their days shall pass away as quickly as shadows because they don't fear God.

* * * * *

14 There is a strange thing happening here upon the

earth: providence seems to treat some good men as though they were wicked, and some wicked men as though they were good. This is all very vexing and troublesome!

*   *   *   *   *

15   Then I decided to spend my time having fun, because I felt that there was nothing better in all the earth than that a man should eat, drink, and be merry, with the hope that this happiness would stick with him in all the hard work which God gives to mankind everywhere.

*   *   *   *   *

16, 17   In my search for wisdom I observed all that was going on everywhere across the earth—ceaseless activity, day and night. (Of course, only God can see everything, and even the wisest man who says he knows everything, doesn't!)

CHAPTER 9

This, too, I carefully explored—that godly and wise men are in God's will; no one knows whether He will favor them or not. All is chance!

2, 3   The same providence confronts everyone, whether good or bad, religious or irreligious, profane or godly. It seems so unfair, that one fate comes to all. That is why men are not more careful to be good, but instead choose their own mad course, for they have no hope—there is nothing but death ahead anyway.

4   There is hope only for the living. "It is better to be a live dog than a dead lion!"

5 For the living at least know that they will die! While the dead know nothing[1]; they don't even have their memories.[1]

6 Whatever they did in their lifetimes—loving, hating, envying—is long gone, and they have no part in anything here on earth any more.

7 So go ahead, eat, drink, and be merry, for it makes no difference to God!

8 Wear fine clothes—with a dash of cologne!

9 Live happily with the woman you love through the fleeting days of life, for the wife God gives you is your best reward down here for all your earthly toil.

10 Whatever you do, do well, for in death, where you are going, there is no working or planning, or knowing, or understanding.[1]

11 Again I looked throughout the earth and saw that the swiftest person does not always win the race, nor the strongest man the battle, and that wise men are often poor, and skillful men are not necessarily famous; but it is all by chance, by happening to be at the right place at the right time.

12 A man never knows when he is going to run into bad luck. He is like a fish caught in a net, or a bird caught in a snare.

*   *   *   *   *

13 Here is another thing that has made a deep impression on me as I have watched human affairs:

14 There was a small city with only a few people living in it, and a great king came with his army and besieged it.

---

[1]These statements are Solomon's discouraged opinion, and do not reflect a knowledge of God's truth on these points!

15   There was in the city a wise man, very poor, and he knew what to do to save the city, and so it was rescued. But afterwards no one thought any more about him.

16   Then I realized that though wisdom is better than strength, nevertheless, if the wise man is poor, he will be despised, and what he says will not be appreciated.

17   But even so, the quiet words of a wise man are better than the shout of a king of fools.

18   Wisdom is better than weapons of war, but one rotten apple can spoil a barrelful.

CHAPTER 10

Dead flies will cause even a bottle of perfume to stink! Yes, a small mistake can outweigh much wisdom and honor.

2   A wise man's heart leads him to do right, and a fool's heart leads him to do evil.

3   You can identify a fool just by the way he walks down the street!

4   If the boss is angry with you, don't quit! A quiet spirit will quiet his bad temper.

5   There is another evil I have seen as I have watched the world go by, a sad situation concerning kings and rulers:

6   For I have seen foolish men given great authority, and rich men not given their rightful place of dignity!

7   I have even seen servants riding, while princes walk like servants!

8, 9   Dig a well—and fall into it!

Demolish an old wall—and be bitten by a snake!

When working in a quarry, stones will fall and crush you! There is risk in each stroke of your axe!

10 A dull axe requires great strength; be wise and sharpen the blade.

11 When the horse is stolen, it is too late to lock the barn.[1]

12, 13 It is pleasant to listen to wise words, but a fool's speech brings him to ruin. Since he begins with a foolish premise, his conclusion is sheer madness.

14 A fool knows all about the future and tells everyone in detail! But who can really know what is going to happen?

15 A fool is so upset by a little work that he has no strength for the simplest matter.[2]

16, 17 Woe to the land whose king is a child and whose leaders are already drunk in the morning. Happy the land whose king is a nobleman, and whose leaders work hard before they feast and drink, and then only to strengthen themselves for the tasks ahead!

18 Laziness lets the roof leak, and soon the rafters begin to rot.

19 A party gives laughter and wine gives happiness, and money gives everything!

20 Never curse the king, not even in your thoughts; nor the rich man either; for a little bird will tell them what you've said.

---

[1] Literally, "If the serpent bites before it is charmed, there is no advantage in a charmer."
[2] Literally, "for a trip to the city."

CHAPTER 11

Give generously, for your gifts will return to you later.

2 Divide your gifts among many,[1] for in the days ahead you yourself may need much help.

3 When the clouds are heavy, the rains come down; when a tree falls, whether south or north, the die is cast, for there it lies.

4 If you wait for perfect conditions, you will never get anything done.[2]

5 God's ways are as mysterious as the pathway of the wind, and as the manner in which a human spirit is infused into the little body of a baby while it is yet in its mother's womb.

6 Keep on sowing your seed, for you never know which will grow—perhaps it all will.

* * * * *

7 It is a wonderful thing to be alive!

8 If a person lives to be very old, let him rejoice in every day of life, but let him also remember that eternity is far longer, and that everything down here is futile in comparison.

* * * * *

9 Young man, it's wonderful to be young! Enjoy every minute of it! Do all you want to; take in everything, but realize that you must account to God for everything you do.

---

[1] Literally, "Give a portion to seven, yes, even to eight."
[2] Literally, "He that observeth the wind shall not sow and he that regardeth the clouds shall not reap."

10 So banish grief and pain, but remember that youth, with a whole life before it, can make serious mistakes.

CHAPTER 12

D on't let the excitement of being young cause you to forget about your Creator. Honor Him in your youth before the evil years come—when you'll no longer enjoy living.

2 It will be too late then to try to remember Him, when the sun and light and moon and stars are dim to your old eyes, and there is no silver lining left among your clouds.

3 For there will come a time when your limbs will tremble with age, and your strong legs will become weak, and your teeth will be too few to do their work, and there will be blindness, too.

4 Then let your lips be tightly closed while eating, when your teeth are gone! And you will waken at dawn with the first note of the birds; but you yourself will be deaf and tuneless, with quavering voice.

5 You will be afraid of heights and of falling—a white-haired, withered old man, dragging himself along: without sexual desire, standing at death's door, and nearing his everlasting home as the mourners go along the streets.

6 Yes, remember your Creator now while you are young, before the silver cord of life snaps, and the golden bowl is broken, and the pitcher is broken at the fountain, and the wheel is broken at the cistern;

7 And the dust returns to the earth as it was, and the spirit returns to God who gave it.

8 All is futile, says the Preacher; utterly futile.

* * * * *

9 But then, because the Preacher was wise, he went on teaching the people all he knew; and he collected proverbs and classified them.

10 For the Preacher was not only a wise man, but a good teacher; he not only taught what he knew to the people, but taught them in an interesting manner.

11 The wise man's words are like goads that spur to action. They nail down important truths. Students are wise who master what their teachers tell them.

12 But my son, be warned: there is no end of opinions ready to be expressed. Studying them can go on forever, and become very exhausting!

13 Here is my final conclusion: fear God and obey His commandments, for this is the entire duty of man.

14 For God will judge us for everything we do, including every hidden thing, good or bad.

The Book of Job

CHAPTER 1

There lived in the land of Uz a man named Job—a good[1] man who feared God and stayed away from evil.

2, 3   He had a large[2] family of seven sons and three daughters, and was immensely wealthy,[2] for he owned 7,000 sheep, 3,000 camels, 500 teams of oxen, 500 female donkeys, and employed many servants. He was, in fact, the richest cattleman in that entire area.

4   Every year when each of Job's sons had a birthday, he invited his brothers and sisters to his home for a celebration. On these occasions they would eat and drink with great merriment.

5   When these birthday parties ended—and sometimes they lasted several days—Job would summon his children to him and sanctify them, getting up early in the morning and offering a burnt offering for each of them. For Job said, "Perhaps my sons have sinned and turned away from God[3] in their hearts." This was Job's regular practice.

*   *   *   *   *

---

[1]Literally, "upright."
[2]Implied.
[3]Literally, "have cursed God."

6   One day as the angels[4] came to present themselves before the Lord, Satan, the Accuser, came with them.

7   "Where have you come from?" the Lord asked Satan. And Satan replied, "From patroling the earth."

8   Then the Lord asked Satan, "Have you noticed my servant Job? He is the finest man in all the earth—a good[5] man who fears God and will have nothing to do with evil."

9   "Why shouldn't he, when you pay him so well?" Satan scoffed.

10   "You have always protected him and his home and his property from all harm. You have prospered everything he does—look how rich he is! No wonder he 'worships' you!

11   But just take away his wealth, and you'll see him curse you to your face!"

12, 13   And the Lord replied to Satan, "You may do anything you like with his wealth, but don't harm him physically."

So Satan went away; and sure enough,[5] not long afterwards when Job's sons and daughters were dining at the oldest brother's house, tragedy struck.

14, 15   A messenger rushed to Job's home with this news: "Your oxen were plowing, with the donkeys feeding beside them, when the Sabeans raided us, drove away the animals and killed all the farmhands except me. I am the only one left."

16   While this messenger was still speaking, another

---

[4]Literally, "the sons of God."
[5]Implied.

arrived with more bad news: "The fire of God has fallen from heaven and burned up your sheep and all the herdsmen, and I alone have escaped to tell you."

17   Before this man finished, still another messenger rushed in: "Three bands of Chaldeans have driven off your camels and killed your servants, and I alone have escaped to tell you."

18   As he was still speaking, another arrived to say, "Your sons and daughters were feasting in their oldest brother's home,

19   When suddenly a mighty wind swept in from the desert, and engulfed the house so that the roof fell in on them and all are dead; and I alone escaped to tell you."

20   Then Job stood up and tore his robe in grief[6] and fell down upon the ground before God.

21   "I came naked from my mother's womb," he said, "And I shall have nothing when I die. The Lord gave me everything I had, and they were His to take away. Blessed be the name of the Lord."

22   In all of this, Job did not sin or revile God.

Chapter 2

Now the angels[1] came again to present themselves before the Lord, and Satan with them.

2   "Where have you come from?" the Lord asked Satan.

"From patroling the earth," Satan replied.

3   "Well, have you noticed My servant Job?" the

---

[6]Literally, "tore his robe and shaved his head."
[1]Literally, "sons of God."

Lord asked. "He is the finest man in all the earth—a good man who fears God and turns away from all evil. And he has kept his faith in Me despite the fact that you persuaded Me to let you harm him without any cause."

4, 5   "Skin for skin," Satan replied. "A man will give anything to save his life. Touch his body with sickness and he will curse You to Your face!"

6   "Do with him as you please," the Lord replied; "only spare his life."

7   So Satan went out from the presence of the Lord and struck Job with a terrible case of boils from head to foot.

8   Then Job took a broken piece of pottery to scrape himself, and sat among the ashes.

9   His wife said to him, "Are you still trying to be godly when God has done all this to you? Curse Him and die."

10   But he replied, "You talk like some heathen woman. What? Shall we receive only pleasant things from the hand of God and never anything unpleasant?" So in all this Job said nothing wrong.

11   When three of Job's friends heard of all the tragedy that had befallen him, they got in touch with each other and traveled from their homes to comfort and console him. Their names were Eliphaz the Temanite, Bildad the Shuhite, and Zophar the Naamathite.

12   Job was so changed that they could scarcely recognize him. Wailing loudly in despair, they tore their robes and threw dust into the air and put earth on their heads to demonstrate their sorrow.

13   Then they sat upon the ground with him silently

for seven days and nights, no one speaking a word; for they saw that his suffering was too great for words.

CHAPTER 3

At last Job spoke, and cursed the day of his birth. 2, 3 "Let the day of my birth be damned," he said, "and the night when I was conceived.

4 Let that day be forever forgotten.[1] Let it be lost even to God, shrouded in eternal darkness.

5 Yes, let the darkness claim it for its own, and may a black cloud overshadow it.

6 May it be blotted off the calendar, never again to be counted among the days of the month of that year.

7 Let that night be bleak and joyless.

8 Let those who are experts at cursing curse it.[2]

9 Let the stars of the night disappear. Let it long for light, but never see it, never see the morning light.

10 Curse it for its failure to shut my mother's womb, for letting me be born to come to all this trouble.

11 Why didn't I die at birth?

12 Why did the midwife let me live? Why did she nurse me at her breasts?

13 For if only I had died at birth, then I would be quiet now, asleep and at rest,

14, 15 Along with prime ministers and kings with all their pomp, and wealthy princes whose castles are full of rich treasures.

---

[1]Literally, "a day of darkness."
[2]Literally, "Let them who can curse the sea, who know how to rouse the sea monster, curse it."

16 Oh, to have been still-born!—to have never breathed or seen the light.

17 For there in death the wicked cease from troubling, and there the weary are at rest.

18 There even prisoners are at ease, with no brutal jailer to curse them.

19 Both rich and poor alike are there, and the slave is free at last from his master.

20, 21 Oh, why should light and life be given to those in misery and bitterness, who long for death, and it won't come; who search for death as others search for food or money!

22 What blessed relief when at last they die!

23 Why is a man allowed to be born if God is only going to give him a hopeless life of uselessness and frustration?

24 I cannot eat for sighing; my groans pour out like water.

25 What I always feared has happened to me.

26 I was not fat and lazy, yet trouble struck me down."

CHAPTER 4

A reply to Job from Eliphaz the Temanite:
2 "Will you let me say a word? For who could keep from speaking out?

3, 4 In the past[1] you have told many a troubled soul to trust in God[2] and have encouraged those who

---

[1]Implied.
[2]Literally, "Thou hast instructed many."

are weak or falling, or lie crushed upon the ground or are tempted to despair.

5   But now, when trouble strikes, you faint and are broken.

6   At such a time as this should not trust in God still be your confidence? Shouldn't you believe that God will care for those who are good?[a]

7, 8   Stop and think! Have you ever known a truly good and innocent person who was punished? Experience teaches that it is those who sow sin and trouble who harvest the same.

9   They die beneath the hand of God.

10   Though they are fierce as young lions, they shall all be broken and destroyed.

11   Like aged, helpless lions they shall starve, and all their children shall be scattered.

*   *   *   *   *

12   This truth was given me in secret, as though whispered in my ear.

13   It came in a nighttime vision as others slept.

14   Suddenly, fear gripped me; I trembled and shook with terror,

15   As a spirit passed before my face—my hair stood up on end.

16   I felt the spirit's presence, but couldn't see it standing there. Then out of the dreadful silence came this voice:

17   'Is mere man more just than God? More pure than his Creator?'

---

[a]Literally, "the integrity of your ways, your hope."

18, 19 If God cannot trust His own messengers (for even angels make mistakes), how much less men made of dust, who are crushed to death as easily as moths!

20 They are alive in the morning, but by evening they are dead, gone forever with hardly a thought from anyone.

21 Their candle of life is snuffed out. They die and no one cares.

CHAPTER 5

They cry for help but no one listens; they turn to their gods, but none gives them aid.

2 They die in helpless frustration, overcome by their own anger.

3 Those who turn from God may be successful for the moment, but then comes sudden disaster.

4 Their children are cheated, with no one to defend them.

5 Their harvests are stolen and their wealth slakes the thirst of many others, not themselves!

6 Misery comes upon them to punish them for sowing seeds of sin.

7 Mankind heads for sin and misery as predictably as flames shoot upwards from a fire.

8 My advice to you is this: Go to God and confess your sins[1] to Him.

9 For He does wonderful miracles, marvels without number.

---

[1]Literally, "I would seek God, and to God would I commit my cause."

10 He sends the rain upon the earth to water the fields,

11 And gives prosperity to the poor and humble, and takes sufferers to safety.

12 He frustrates the plans of crafty men.

13 They are caught in their own traps; He thwarts their schemes.

14 They grope like blind men in the daylight; they see no better in the daytime than at night.

15 God saves the fatherless and the poor from the grasp of these oppressors.

16 And so at last the poor have hope, and the fangs of the wicked are broken.

17 How enviable the man whom God corrects! Oh, do not despise the chastening of the Lord when you sin.

18 For though He wounds, He binds and heals again.

19 He will deliver you again and again, so that no evil can touch you.

20 He will keep you from death in famine, and from the power of the sword in time of war.

21 You will be safe from slander; no need to fear the future.

22 You shall laugh at war and famine; wild animals will leave you alone.

23 Dangerous animals will be at peace with you.

24 You need not worry about your home while you are gone; nothing shall be stolen from your barns.

25 Your sons shall become important men; your descendants shall be as numerous as grass!

26 You shall live a long, good life; like standing grain, you'll not be harvested until it's time!

27 I have found from experience that all of this is true. For your own good, listen to my counsel."

CHAPTER 6

J*ob's reply:*
2 "Oh, that my sadness and troubles were weighed.

3 For they are heavier than the sand of a thousand seashores. That is why I spoke so rashly.

4 For the Lord has struck me down with His arrows; He has sent His poisoned arrows deep within my heart. All God's terrors are arrayed against me.

5, 6, 7 When wild donkeys bray, it is because their grass is gone; oxen do not low when they have food; a man complains when there is no salt in his food. And how tasteless is the uncooked white of an egg—my appetite is gone when I look at it; I gag at the thought of eating it!

8, 9 Oh, that God would grant the thing I long for most—to die beneath His hand, and be freed from His painful grip.

10 This, at least, gives me comfort despite all the pain—that I have not denied the words of the holy God.

11 Oh, why does my strength sustain me? How can I be patient till I die?

12 Am I unfeeling, like stone? Is my flesh made of brass?

13 For I am utterly helpless, without any hope.

14   One should be kind to a fainting friend, but you have accused me without the slightest fear of God.

15-18   My brother, you have proved as unreliable as a brook; it floods when there is ice and snow, but in hot weather, disappears. The caravans turn aside to be refreshed, but there is nothing there to drink, and so they perish.

19-21   When caravans from Tema and from Sheba stop for water there, their hopes are dashed. And so my hopes in you are dashed—you turn away from me in terror and refuse to help.

22   But why? Have I ever asked you for one slightest thing? Have I begged you for a present?

23   Have I ever asked your help?

24   All I want is a reasonable answer—then I will keep quiet. Tell me, what have I done wrong?

25, 26   It is wonderful to speak the truth, but your criticisms are not based on fact. Are you going to condemn me just because I impulsively cried out in desperation?

27   That would be like injuring a helpless orphan, or selling a friend.

28   Look at me! Would I lie to your face?

29   Stop assuming my guilt, for I am righteous. Don't be so unjust.

30   Don't I know the difference between right and wrong? Would I not admit it if I had sinned?

CHAPTER 7

How mankind must struggle. A man's life is long and hard, like that of a slave.

2   How he longs for the day to end. How he grinds on to the end of the week and his wages.

3   And so to me also have been allotted months of frustration, these long and weary nights.

4   When I go to bed I think, 'Oh, that it were morning' and then I toss till dawn.

5   My skin is filled with worms and blackness. My flesh breaks open, full of pus.

6   My life flies by—day after hopeless day.

7   My life is but a breath, and nothing good is left.

8   You see me now, but not for long. Soon you'll look upon me dead.

9   As a cloud disperses and vanishes, so those who die shall go away forever—

10   Gone forever from their family and their home—never to be seen again.

11   Ah, let me express my anguish. Let me be free to speak out of the bitterness of my soul.

12   O God, am I some monster, that You never let me alone?

13, 14   Even when I try to forget my misery in sleep, You terrify with nightmares.

15   I would rather die of strangulation than go on and on like this.

16   I hate my life. Oh, let me alone for these few remaining days.

17 What is mere man that You should spend Your time persecuting him?

18 Must You be his inquisitor every morning, and test him every moment of the day?

19 Why won't You let me alone—even long enough to spit?

20 Has my sin harmed You, O God, Watcher of Mankind? Why have You made me Your target, and made my life so heavy a burden to me?

21 Why not just pardon my sin and take it all away? For all so soon I'll lie down in the dust and die, and when You look for me, I shall be gone."

CHAPTER 8

Bildad the Shuhite replies to Job:
2 "How long will you go on like this, Job, blowing words around like wind?

3 Does God twist justice?

4 If your children sinned against Him, and He punished them,

5 And you begged Almighty God for them—

6 If you were pure and good, He would hear your prayer, and answer you, and bless you with a happy home.

7 And though you started with little, you would end with much.

8 Read the history books and see—

9 For we were born but yesterday and know so little; our days here on earth are as transient as shadows.

10 But the wisdom of the past will teach you. The experience of others will speak to you, reminding you that

11-13 Those who forget God have no hope. They are like rushes without any mire to grow in; or grass without water to keep it alive. Suddenly it begins to wither, even before it is cut.

14 A man without God is trusting in a spider's web. Everything he counts on will collapse.

15 If he counts on his home for security, it won't last.

16 At dawn he seems so strong and virile, like a green plant; his branches spread across the garden.

17 His roots are in the stream, down among the stones.

18 But when he disappears, he isn't even missed!

19 That is all he can look forward to! And others spring up from the earth to replace him!

20 But look! God will not cast away a good man, nor prosper evildoers.

21 He will yet fill your mouth with laughter and your lips with shouts of joy.

22 Those who hate you shall be clothed with shame, and the wicked destroyed."

CHAPTER 9

Job's reply:

2 "Sure, I know all that. You're not telling me anything new. But how can a man be truly good in the eyes of God?

3 If God decides to argue with him, can a man answer even one question of a thousand He asks?

4 For God is so wise and so mighty. Who has ever opposed Him successfully?

5 Suddenly He moves the mountains, overturning them in His anger.

6 He shakes the earth to its foundations.

7 The sun won't rise, the stars won't shine, if He commands it so!

8 Only He has stretched the heavens out and stalked along the seas.

9 He made the Bear, Orion and the Pleiades, and the constellations of the southern Zodiac.

10 He does incredible miracles, too many to count.

11 He passes by, invisible; He moves along, but I don't see Him go.

12 When He sends death to snatch a man away,[1] who can stop him? Who dares to ask Him, 'What are You doing?'

13 And God does not abate His anger. The pride of man[2] collapses before Him.

14 And who am I that I should try to argue with Almighty God, or even reason with Him?

15 Even if I were sinless I wouldn't say a word. I would only plead for mercy.

16 And even if my prayers were answered I could scarce believe that He had heard my cry.

---

[1]Literally, "He seizes."
[2]Or, "the helpers of Rahab."

17 For He is the one who destroys, and multiplies my wounds without a cause.

18 He will not let me breathe, but fills me with bitter sorrows.

19 He alone is strong and just.

20 But I? Am I righteous? My own mouth says no. Even if I were perfect, God would prove me wicked.

21 And even if I am utterly innocent, I dare not think of it. I despise what I am.

22 Innocent or evil, it is all the same to Him. For He destroys both kinds.

23 He will laugh when calamity crushes the innocent.

24 The whole earth is in the hands of the wicked. God blinds the eyes of the judges and lets them be unfair. If not He, then who?

25 My life passes swiftly away, filled with tragedy.

26 My years disappear like swift ships, like the eagle that swoops upon its prey.

27 If I decided to forget my complaints against God, to end my sadness and be cheerful,

28 Then He would pour even greater sorrows upon me. For I know that You will not hold me innocent, O God,

29 But will condemn me. So what's the use of trying?

30 Even if I were to wash myself with purest water and cleanse my hands with lye to make them utterly clean,

31 Even so You would plunge me into the ditch and

mud; and even my clothing would be less filthy than You consider me to be!

32, 33   And I cannot defend myself, for You are no mere man as I am. If You were, then we could discuss it fairly, but there is no umpire between us, no middle man, no mediator to bring us together.

34   Oh, let Him stop beating me, so that I need no longer live in terror of His punishment.

35   Then I could speak without fear to Him, and tell Him boldly that I am not guilty.

CHAPTER 10

I am weary of living. Let me complain freely. I will speak in my sorrow and bitterness.

2   I will say to God, Don't just condemn me—tell me *why* You are doing it.

3   Does it really seem right to You to oppress and despise me, a man You have made; and to send joy and prosperity to the wicked?

4-7   Are You unjust[1] like men? Is Your life so short that You must hound me for sins You know full well I've not committed? Is it because You know no one can save me from Your hand?

8   You have made me, and yet You destroy me.

9   Oh, please remember that I'm made of dust—will You change me back again to dust so soon?

10   You have already poured me from bottle to bottle like milk, and curdled me like cheese.

---

[1]Literally, "Have You the eyes of flesh?"

11   You gave me skin and flesh and knit together bones and sinews.

12   You gave me life and were so kind and loving to me, and I was preserved by Your care.

13, 14   Yet all the time Your real motive in making me was to destroy me if I sinned; and to refuse to forgive my iniquity.

15   Just the slightest wickedness, and I am done for. And if I'm good, that doesn't count. I am filled with frustration.

16   If I start to get up off the ground, You leap upon me like a lion and quickly finish me off.

17   Again and again You witness against me and pour out an ever-increasing volume of wrath upon me and bring fresh armies against me.

18   Why then did You even let me be born? Why didn't You let me die at birth?

19   Then I would have been spared this miserable existence. I would have gone directly from the womb to the grave.

20, 21   Can't You see how little time I have left? Oh, let me alone that I may have a little moment of comfort before I leave for the land of darkness and the shadow of death, never to return;

22   A land as dark as midnight; a land of the shadow of death where only confusion reigns, and where the brightest light is dark as midnight."

CHAPTER 11

Zophar the Naamathite replies to Job:

2   "Shouldn't someone stem this torrent of words? Is a man proved right by all this talk?

3   Should I remain silent while you boast? When you mock God, shouldn't someone make you ashamed?

4   You claim you are pure in the eyes of God!

5   Oh, that God would speak and tell you what He thinks!

6   Oh, that He would make you truly see yourself, for He knows everything you've done. Listen! God is doubtless punishing you far less than you deserve!

7   Do you know the mind and purposes of God? Will long searching make them known to you? Are you qualified to judge the Almighty?

8   He is as faultless as heaven is high—but who are you? His mind is fathomless—what can you know in comparison?

9   His spirit is broader than the earth and wider than the sea.

10   If He rushes in and makes an arrest, and calls the court to order, who is going to stop Him?

11   For He knows perfectly all the faults and sins of mankind; He sees all sin without searching.

12   Mere man is as likely to be wise as a wild donkey's colt is likely to be born a man!

13, 14   Before you turn to God and stretch out your hands to Him, get rid of your sins and leave all iniquity behind you.

15 Only then, without the spots of sin to defile you, can you walk steadily forward to God without fear.

16 Only then can you forget your misery. It will all be in the past.

17 And your life will be cloudless; any darkness will be as bright as morning!

18 You will have courage because you will have hope. You will take your time, and rest in safety.

19 You will lie down unafraid and many will look to you for help.

20 But the wicked shall find no way to escape; their only hope is death."

CHAPTER 12

Job's reply:

2 "Yes, I realize you know everything! All wisdom will die with you!

3 Well, I know a few things myself—you are no better than I am. And who doesn't know these things you've been saying?

4 I, the man who begged God for help, and God answered him, have become a laughingstock to my neighbors. Yes, I, a righteous man, am now the man they scoff at.

5 Meanwhile, the rich mock those in trouble and are quick to despise all those in need.

6 For robbers prosper. Go ahead and provoke God —it makes no difference! He will supply your every need anyway!

7, 8, 9   Who doesn't know that the Lord does things like that? Ask the dumbest beast—he knows that it is so; ask the birds—they will tell you; or let the earth teach you, or the fish of the sea.

10   For the soul of every living thing is in the hand of God, and the breath of all mankind.

11   Just as my mouth can taste good food, so my mind tastes truth when I hear it.

12   And as you say, older men like me[1] are wise. They understand.

13   But true wisdom and power are God's. He alone knows what we should do; He understands.

14   And how great is His might! What He destroys can't be rebuilt. When He closes in on a man, there is no escape.

15   He withholds the rain, and the earth becomes a desert; He sends the storms, and floods the ground.

16   Yes, with Him is strength and wisdom. Deceivers and deceived are both His slaves.

17   He makes fools of counselors and judges.

18   He reduces kings to slaves and frees their servants.

19   Priests are led away as slaves. He overthrows the mighty.

20   He takes away the voice of orators, and the insight of the elders.

21   He pours contempt upon princes, and weakens the strong.

22   He floods the darkness with light, even the dark shadow of death.

---

[1]Implied.

23 He raises up a nation and then destroys it. He makes it great, and then reduces it to nothing.

24, 25 He takes away the understanding of presidents and kings, and leaves them wandering, lost and groping, without a guiding light.

CHAPTER 13

Look, I have seen many instances like you describe. I understand what you are saying.

2 I know as much as you do. I'm not stupid.

3 Oh, how I long to speak directly to the Almighty. I want to talk this over with God Himself.

4 For you are misinterpreting the whole thing. You are doctors who don't know what they are doing.

5 Oh, please be quiet! That would be your highest wisdom.

6 Listen to me now, to my reasons for what I think, and to my pleadings.

7 Must you go on 'speaking for God' when He never once has said the things that you are putting in His mouth?

8 Does God want your help if you are going to twist the truth for Him?

9 Be careful that He doesn't find out what you are doing! Or do you think you can fool God as well as men?

10 No, you will be in serious trouble with Him if you use lies to try to help Him out.

11 Doesn't His majesty strike terror to your heart? How can you do this thing?

12   These tremendous statements you have made
have about as much value as ashes. Your defense of
God is as fragile as a clay vase!

13   Be silent now and let me alone, that I may speak
—and I am willing to face the consequences.

14   Yes, I will take my life in my hand and say what
I really think.

15   God may kill me for saying this—in fact, I expect Him to. Nevertheless I am going to argue my case
with Him.[1]

16   This at least will be in my favor, that I am not
godless, to be rejected instantly from His presence.

17   Listen closely to what I am about to say. Hear
me out.

18   This is my case: *I know that I am righteous.*

19   Who can argue with me over this? If you could
prove me wrong I would stop defending myself and die.

20   O God, there are two things I beg You not to do
to me; only then will I be able to face You.

21   Don't abandon me. And don't terrify me with
Your awesome presence.

22   Call to me to come—how quickly I will answer!
Or let me speak to You, and You reply.

23   Tell me, what have I done wrong? Help me!
Point out my sin to me.

24   Why do You turn away from me? Why hand me
over to my enemy?

25   Would You blame a leaf that is blown about by
the wind? Will You chase dry, useless straws?

---

[1]Or, "Though He slay me, yet will I trust in Him. I will argue my case
before Him."

26 You write bitter things against me and bring up all the follies of my youth.

27, 28 You send me to prison and shut me in on every side. I am like a fallen, rotten tree, like a moth-eaten coat.

CHAPTER 14

How frail is man, how few his days, how full of trouble!

2 He blossoms for a moment like a flower—and withers; as the shadow of a passing cloud, he quickly disappears.

3 Must You be so harsh with frail men, and demand an accounting from them?

4 How can You demand purity in one born impure?

5 You have set mankind so brief a span of life—months is all You give him! Not one bit longer may he live.

6 So give him a little rest, won't You? Turn away Your angry gaze and let him have a few moments of relief before he dies.

7 For there is hope for a tree—if it's cut down it sprouts again, and grows tender, new branches.

8, 9 Though its roots have grown old in the earth, and its stump decays, it may sprout and bud again at the touch of water, like a new seedling.

10 But when a man dies and is buried, where does his spirit go?

11, 12 As water evaporates from a lake, as a river disappears in drought, so a man lies down for the last time, and does not rise again until the heavens are no more; he shall not awaken, nor be roused from his sleep.

13 Oh, that You would hide me with the dead, and forget me there until Your anger ends; but mark Your calendar to think of me again!

14 If a man dies, shall he live again? This thought gives me hope, so that in all my anguish I eagerly await sweet death!

15 You would call and I would come, and You would reward all I do.

16 But now, instead, You give me so few steps upon the stage of life, and notice every mistake I make.

17 You bundle them all together as evidence against me.

18, 19 Mountains wear away and disappear. Water grinds the stones to sand. Torrents tear away the soil. So every hope of man is worn away.

20, 21 Always You are against him, and then he passes off the scene. You make him old and wrinkled, then send him away. He never knows it if his sons are honored; or they may fail and face disaster, but he knows it not.

22 For him there is only sorrow and pain.

CHAPTER 15

The answer of Eliphaz the Temanite:

2 "You are supposed to be a wise man, and yet you give us all this foolish talk. You are nothing but a windbag.

3 It isn't right to speak so foolishly. What good do such words do?

4, 5   Have you no fear of God? No reverence for Him? Your sins are telling your mouth what to say! Your words are based on clever deception,

6   But why should I condemn you? Your own mouth does!

7, 8   Are you the wisest man alive? Were you born before the hills were made? Have you heard the secret counsel of God? Are you called into His counsel room? Do you have a monopoly on wisdom?

9   What do you know more than we do? What do you understand that we don't?

10   On our side are aged men much older than your father!

11   Is God's comfort too little for you? Is His gentleness too rough?

12   What is this you are doing, getting carried away by your anger, with flashing eyes?

13   And you turn against God and say all these evil things against Him.

14   What man in all the earth can be as pure and righteous as you claim to be?

15   Why, God doesn't even trust the angels! Even the heavens can't be absolutely pure compared with Him!

16   How much less someone like you, who is corrupt and sinful, drinking in sin as a sponge soaks up water!

17-19   Listen, and I will answer you from my own experience, confirmed by the experience of wise men who have been told this same thing from their fathers— our ancestors to whom alone the land was given—and they have passed this wisdom to us:

20   A wicked man is always in trouble throughout his life.

21   He is surrounded by terrors, and if there are good days they will soon be gone.

22   He dares not go out into the darkness, lest he be murdered.

23, 24   He wanders around begging for food. He lives in fear, distress, and anguish. His enemies conquer him as a king defeats his foes.

25, 26   Armed with his tin shield he clenches his fist against God, defying the Almighty, stubbornly assaulting Him.

27, 28   This wicked man is fat and rich, and has lived in conquered cities after killing off its citizens.

29   But he will not continue to be rich, or to extend his possessions.

30   No, darkness shall overtake him forever; the breath of God shall destroy him; the flames shall burn up all he has.

31   Let him no longer trust in foolish riches; let him no longer deceive himself, for the money he trusts in will be his only reward.

32   Before he dies, all this futility will become evident to him. For all he counted on will disappear,

33   And fall to the ground like a withered grape.[2] How little will come of his hopes!

34   For the godless are barren: they can produce nothing truly good. God's fire consumes them with all their possessions.

---

[1]Literally, "trust in vanity."
[2]Literally, "shall cast off his flower as the olive tree."

35   The only thing they can 'conceive' is sin, and their hearts give birth only to wickedness."

CHAPTER 16

Job's reply:

2   "I have heard all this before. What miserable comforters all of you are.

3   Won't you ever stop your flow of foolish words? What have I said that makes you speak so endlessly?

4   But perhaps I'd sermonize the same as you—if you were I and I were you. I would spout off my criticisms against you and shake my head at you.

5   But no! I would speak in such a way that it would help you. I would try to take away your grief.

6   But now my grief remains no matter how I defend myself; nor does it help if I refuse to speak.

7   For God has ground me down, and taken away my family.

8   O God, You have turned me to skin and bones— as a proof, they say, of my sins.

9   God hates me and angrily tears at my flesh; He has gnashed upon me with His teeth, and watched to snuff out any sign of life.

10   These 'comforters' have gaping jaws to swallow me; they slap my cheek. My enemies gather themselves against me.

11   And God has delivered me over to sinners, into the hands of the wicked.

12   I was living quietly until He broke me apart. He

has taken me by the neck and dashed me to pieces, then hung me up as His target.

13 His archers surround me, letting fly their arrows, so that the ground is wet from my wounds.

14 Again and again He attacks me, running upon me like a giant.

15 Here I sit in sackcloth; and have laid all hope in the dust.

16 My eyes are red with weeping and on my eyelids is the shadow of death.

17 Yet I am innocent, and my prayer is pure.

18 O earth, do not conceal my blood. Let it protest on my behalf.

19 Yet even now the Witness to my innocence is there in heaven; my Advocate is there on high.

20 My friends scoff at me, but I pour out my tears to God,

21 Pleading that He will listen as a man would listen to his neighbor.

22 For all so soon I must go down that road from which I shall never return.

CHAPTER 17

I am sick and near to death; the grave is ready to receive me.

2 I am surrounded by mockers. I see them everywhere.

3, 4 Will no one anywhere confirm my innocence? But You, O God, have kept them back from understanding this. Oh, do not let them triumph.

5 If they accept bribes to denounce their friends, their children shall go blind.

6 He has made me a mockery among the people; they spit in my face.

7 My eyes are dim with weeping and I am but a shadow of my former self.

8 Fair-minded men are astonished when they see me. Yet, finally, the innocent shall come out on top, above the godless;

9 The righteous shall move onward and forward; those with pure hearts shall become stronger and stronger.

10 As for you—all of you please go away; for I do not find a wise man among you.

11 My good days are in the past. My hopes have disappeared. My heart's desires are broken.

12 They say that night is day and day is night; how they pervert the truth!

13, 14 If I die, I go out into darkness, and call the grave my father, and the worm my mother and my sister.

15 Where then is my hope? Can anyone find any?

16 No, my hope will go down with me to the grave. We shall rest together in the dust!"

CHAPTER 18

The further reply of Bildad the Shuhite:

2 "Who are you trying to fool? Speak some sense if you want us to answer!

3   Have we become like animals to you, stupid and dumb?

4   Just because you tear your clothes in anger, is this going to start an earthquake? Shall we all go and hide?

5   The truth remains that if you do not prosper, it is because you are wicked. And your bright flame shall be put out.

6   There will be darkness in every home where there is wickedness.

7   The confident stride of the wicked man will be shortened; he will realize his failing strength.

8, 9   He walks into traps, and robbers will ambush him.

10   There is a booby-trap in every path he takes.

11   He has good cause for fear—his enemy is close behind him!

12   His vigor is depleted by hunger; calamity stands ready to pounce upon him.

13   His skin is eaten by disease. Death shall devour him.

14   The wealth he trusted in shall reject him, and he shall be brought down to the King of Terrors.

15   His home shall disappear beneath a fiery barrage of brimstone.

16   He shall die from the roots up, and all his branches will be lopped off.

17   All memory of his existence will perish from the earth; no one will remember him.

18   He will be driven out from the kingdom of light into darkness, and chased out of the world.

19 He will have neither son nor grandson left, nor any other relatives.

20 Old and young alike will be horrified by his fate.

21 Yes, that is what happens to sinners, to those rejecting God."

CHAPTER 19

he reply of Job:

2 "How long are you going to trouble me, and try to break me with your words?

3 Ten times now you have declared I am a sinner. Why aren't you ashamed to deal with me so harshly?

4 And if indeed I was wrong, you have yet to prove it.

5 You think yourselves so great? Then prove my guilt!

6 The fact of the matter is that God has overthrown me and caught me in His net.

7 I scream for help and no one hears me. I shriek, but get no justice.

8 God has blocked my path and turned my light to darkness.

9 He has stripped me of my glory and removed the crown from my head.

10 He has broken me down on every side, and I am done for. He has destroyed all hope.

11 His fury burns against me; He counts me as an enemy.

12 He sends His troops to surround my tent.

13 He has sent away my brothers, and my friends.

14 My relatives have failed me; my friends have all forsaken me.

15 Those living in my home, even my servants, regard me as a stranger. I am like a foreigner to them.

16 I call my servant, but he doesn't come; I even beg him!

17 My own wife and brothers refuse to recognize me.

18 Even young children despise me. When I stand to speak, they mock.

19 My best friends abhor me. Those I loved have turned against me.

20 I am skin and bones and have escaped death by the skin of my teeth.

21 Oh, my friends, pity me, for the angry hand of God has touched me.

22 Why must you persecute me as God does? Why aren't you satisfied with my anguish?

23, 24 Oh, that I could write my plea with an iron pen in the rock forever.

25 But as for me, I know that my Redeemer lives, and that He will stand upon the earth at last.

26 And I know that after this body has decayed, this body shall see God![1]

27 Then He will be on *my* side! Yes, I shall see Him, not as a stranger, but as a friend! What a glorious hope!

28 How dare you go on persecuting me, as though I were proven guilty?

---

[1]Or, "then even without my flesh I shall see God."

29   I warn you, you yourselves are in danger of punishment for your attitude."

CHAPTER 20

The speech of Zophar the Naamathite:
2   "I hasten to reply. For I have the answer for you.

3   You have tried to make me feel ashamed of myself for calling you a sinner, but my spirit won't let me stop.

4   Don't you realize that ever since man was first placed upon the earth,

5   The triumph of the wicked has been short-lived, and the joy of the godless but for a moment?

6   Though the godless be proud as the heavens, and walk with his nose in the air,

7   Yet he shall perish forever, cast away like his own dung. Those who knew him will wonder where he is gone.

8   He will fade like a dream.

9   Neither his friends nor his family will ever see him again.

10   His children shall beg from the poor, their hard labor shall repay his debts.

11   Though still a young man, his bones shall lie in the dust.

12   He enjoyed the taste of his wickedness, letting it melt in his mouth,

13   Sipping it slowly, lest it disappear.

14 But suddenly the food he has eaten turns sour within him.

15 He will vomit the plunder he gorged. God won't let him keep it down.

16 It is like poison and death to him.

17 He shall not enjoy the goods he stole; they will not be butter and honey to him after all.

18 His labors shall not be rewarded; wealth will give him no joy.

19 For he has oppressed the poor and foreclosed their homes; he will never recover.

20 Though he was always greedy, now he has nothing; of all the things he dreamed of—none remain.

21 Because he stole at every opportunity, his prosperity shall not continue.

22 He shall run into trouble at the peak of his powers; all the wicked shall destroy him.

23 Just as he is about to fill his belly, God will rain down wrath upon him.

24 He will be chased and struck down.

25 The arrow is pulled from his body—and the glittering point comes out from his gall. The terrors of death are upon him.

26 His treasures will be lost in deepest darkness. A raging fire will devour his goods, consuming all he has left.

27 The heavens will reveal his sins, and the earth will give testimony against him.

28 His wealth will disappear beneath the wrath of God.

29   This is what awaits the wicked man, for God prepares it for him."

CHAPTER 21

Job's reply:

2, 3   "Listen to me; let me speak, and afterwards, mock on.

4   I am complaining about God,[1] not man; no wonder my spirit is so troubled.

5   Look at me in horror, and lay your hand upon your mouth.

6   Even I am frightened when I see myself. Horror takes hold upon me and I shudder.

7   The truth is that the wicked live on to a good old age, and become great and powerful.

8   They live to see their children grow to maturity around them, and their grandchildren, too.

9   Their homes are safe from every fear, and God does not punish them.

10   Their cattle are productive:

11   They have many happy children,

12, 13   They spend their time singing and dancing. They are wealthy and need deny themselves nothing; they are prosperous to the end.

14   All this despite the fact that they ordered God away and wanted no part of Him and His ways.

15   'Who is Almighty God?' they scoff; 'Why should we obey him? What good will it do us?'

---

[1]Implied.

16   Look, everything the wicked touch has turned to gold! But I refuse even to deal with people like that.

17   Yet the wicked get away with it every time. They never have trouble, and God skips them when He distributes His sorrows and anger.

18   Are they driven before the wind like straw? Are they carried away by the storm? Not at all!

19   'Well,' you say, 'at least God will punish their children!' But I say that God should punish the man who sins, not his children! Let him feel the penalty himself.

20   Yes, let him be destroyed for his iniquity. Let him drink deeply of the anger of the Almighty.

21   For when he is dead, then he will never again be able to enjoy his family.

22   But who can rebuke God, the supreme Judge?

23, 24   He destroys those who are healthy, wealthy, fat, and prosperous;

25   God also destroys those in deep and grinding poverty who have never known anything good.

26   Both alike are buried in the same dust, both eaten by the same worms.

27   I know what you are going to say—

28   You will tell me of rich and wicked men who came to disaster because of their sins.

29   But I reply, Ask anyone who has been around and he can tell you the truth,

30-32   That the evil man is usually spared in the day of calamity, and allowed to escape. No one rebukes him openly. No one repays him for what he has done. And an honor-guard keeps watch at his grave.

33　A great funeral procession precedes and follows him as the soft earth covers him.

34　How can you comfort me when your whole premise is so wrong?"

CHAPTER 22

Another address from Eliphaz:

2　"Is mere man of any worth to God? Even the wisest is of value only to himself!

3　Is it any pleasure to the Almighty if you are righteous? Would it be any gain to Him if you were perfect?

4　Is it because you are good that He is punishing you?

5　Not at all! It is because of your wickedness! Your sins are endless!

6　For instance, you must have refused to loan money to needy friends unless they gave you all their clothing as a pledge—yes, you must have stripped them to the bone.

7　You must have refused water to the thirsty, and bread to the starving.

8　But no doubt you gave men of importance anything they wanted, and let the wealthy live wherever they chose.

9　You sent widows away without helping them, and broke the arms of orphans.

10, 11　That is why you are now surrounded by traps and sudden fears, and darkness and waves of horror.

12　God is so great—higher than the heavens, higher than the stars.

13　But you reply, 'That is why He can't see what I am doing! How can He judge through the thick darkness?

14　For thick clouds swirl about Him so that He cannot see us. He is way up there, walking on the vault of heaven.'

15, 16　Don't you realize that those treading the ancient paths of sin are snatched away in youth, and the foundations of their lives washed out forever?

17　For they said to God, 'Go away, God! What can You do for us?'

18　(God forbid that I should say a thing like that.) Yet they forgot that He had filled their homes with good things.

19　And now the righteous shall see them destroyed; the innocent shall laugh the wicked to scorn.

20　'See,' they will say, 'the last of our enemies have been destroyed in the fire.'

21　Quit quarreling with God! Agree with Him and you will have peace at last! His favor will surround you if you will only admit that you were wrong.

22　Listen to His instructions and store them in your heart.

23　If you return to God and put right all the wrong in your home, then you will be restored.

24　If you give up your lust for money, and throw your gold away,

25　Then the Almighty Himself shall be your treasure; He will be your precious silver!

26 Then you will delight yourself in the Lord, and look up to God.

27 You will pray to Him, and He will hear you, and you will fulfill all your promises to Him.

28 Whatever you wish will happen! and the light of heaven will shine upon the road ahead of you.

29 If you are attacked and knocked down, you will know that there is someone who will lift you up again. Yes, He will save the humble,

30 And help even sinners by your pure hands."

CHAPTER 23

The reply of Job:

2 "My complaint today is still a bitter one, and my punishment far more severe than my fault deserves.

3 Oh, that I knew where to find God—that I could go to His throne and talk with Him there.

4, 5 I would tell Him all about my side of this argument, and listen to His reply, and understand what He wants.

6 Would He merely overpower me with His greatness? No, He would listen with sympathy.

7 Fair and honest men could reason with Him, and be acquitted by my Judge.

8 But I search in vain. I seek Him here, I seek Him there, and cannot find Him.

9 I seek Him in His workshop in the North, but cannot find Him there; nor can I find Him in the South; there, too, He hides Himself.

10 But He knows every detail of what is happening

to me; and when He has examined me, He will pronounce me completely innocent—as pure as solid gold!

11 I have stayed in God's paths, following His steps. I have not turned aside.

12 I have not refused His commandments but have enjoyed them more than my daily food.

13 Nevertheless, His mind concerning me remains unchanged, and who can turn Him from His purposes? Whatever He wants to do, He does.

14 So He will do to me all He has planned, and there is more ahead.[1]

15 No wonder I am so terrified in His presence. When I think of it, terror grips me.

16, 17 God has given me a fainting heart; He, the Almighty, has terrified me with darkness all around me; thick, impenetrable darkness everywhere.

CHAPTER 24

Why doesn't God open the court and listen to my case? Why must the godly wait for Him in vain?

2 For a crime wave has engulfed us—landmarks are moved, flocks of sheep are stolen,

3 And even the donkeys of the poor and fatherless are taken. Poor widows must surrender the little they have as a pledge to get a loan.

4 The needy are kicked aside; they must get out of the way.

5 Like the wild donkeys in the desert, the poor must spend all their time just getting barely enough to keep

---

[1]Literally, "and many such things are with Him."

soul and body together. They are sent into the desert to search for food for their children.

6   They eat what they find that grows wild, and must even glean the vineyards of the wicked.

7   All night they lie naked in the cold, without clothing or covering.

8   They are wet with the showers of the mountains and live in caves for want of a home.

9   The wicked snatch fatherless children from their mother's breasts, and take a poor man's baby as a pledge before they will loan him any money or grain.

10   That is why they must go about naked, without clothing, and are forced to carry food while they are starving.

11   They are forced to press out the olive oil without tasting it, and to tread out the grape juice as they suffer from thirst.

12   The bones of the dying cry from the city; the wounded cry for help; yet God does not respond to their moaning.

13   The wicked rebel against the light and are not acquainted with the right and the good.

14, 15   They are murderers who rise in the early dawn to kill the poor and needy; at night they are thieves and adulterers, waiting for the twilight 'when no one will see me,' they say. They mask their faces so no one will know them.

16   They break into houses at night and sleep in the daytime—they are not acquainted with the light.

17   The black night is their morning; they ally themselves with the terrors of the darkness.

18   But how quickly they disappear from the face of the earth. Everything they own is cursed. They leave no property for their children.

19   Death consumes sinners like drought and heat consume snow.

20   Even the sinner's own mother shall forget him. Worms shall feed sweetly on him. No one will remember him any more. For wicked men are broken like a tree in the storm.

21   For they have taken advantage of the childless who have no protecting sons. They refuse to help the needy widows.

22, 23   Yet sometimes[1] it seems as though God preserves the rich by His power, and restores them to life when anyone else would die. God gives them confidence and strength, and helps them in many ways.

24   But though they are very great now, yet in a moment they shall be gone like all others, cut off like heads of grain.

25   Can anyone claim otherwise? Who can prove me a liar and claim that I am wrong?"

Chapter 25

The further reply of Bildad the Shuhite:
2   "God is powerful and dreadful. He enforces peace in heaven.

3   Who is able to number His hosts of angels? And His light shines down on all the earth.

4   How can mere man stand before God and claim

---

[1]Implied.

to be righteous? Who in all the earth can boast that he is clean?

5   God is so glorious that even the moon and stars are less than nothing as compared to Him.

6   How much less is man, who is but a worm in His sight?"

CHAPTER 26

Job's reply:

2   "What wonderful helpers you all are! And how you have encouraged me in my great need!

3   How you have enlightened my stupidity! What wise things you have said!

4   How did you ever think of all these brilliant comments?

5, 6   The dead stand naked, trembling before God in the place where they go.

7   God stretches out Heaven over empty space, and hangs the earth upon nothing.

8   He wraps the rain in His thick clouds and the clouds are not split by the weight.

9   He shrouds His throne with His clouds.

10   He sets a boundary for the ocean, yes, and a boundary for the day and for the night.

11   The pillars of heaven tremble at His rebuke.

12   And by His power the sea grows calm; He is skilled at crushing its pride!

13   The heavens are made beautiful by His Spirit;[1] He pierces the swiftly gliding serpent.

---

[1]Or, "the bars of heaven are afraid of Him." See verse 11.

14   These are some of the minor things He does, merely a whisper of His power. Who then can withstand His thunder?"

CHAPTER 27

Job's final defense:

2   "I vow by the living God, who has taken away my rights, even the Almighty God who has embittered my soul,

3   That as long as I live, while I have breath from God,

4   My lips shall speak no evil, my tongue shall speak no lies.

5   I will never, never agree that you are right; until I die I will vow my innocence.

6   I am *not* a sinner—I repeat it again and again. My conscience is clear for as long as I live.

7   Those who declare otherwise are my wicked enemies. They are evil men.

8   But what hope has the godless when God cuts him off and takes away his life?

9   Will God listen to his cry when trouble comes upon him?

10   For he does not delight himself in the Almighty or pay any attention to God except in times of crisis.

11   I will teach you about God—

12   But really, I don't need to, for you yourselves know as much about Him as I do; yet you are saying all these useless things to me.

13　This is the fate awaiting the wicked from the hand of the Almighty:

14　If he has a multitude of children, it is so that they will die in war, or starve to death.

15　Those who survive shall be brought down to the grave by disease and plague, with no one to mourn them, not even their wives.

16　The evil man may accumulate money like dust, with closets jammed full of clothing—

17　Yes, he may order them made by his tailor, but the innocent shall wear that clothing, and shall divide his silver among them.

18　Every house built by the wicked is as fragile as a spider web; as full of cracks as a leafy booth!

19　He goes to bed rich, but wakes up to find that all his wealth is gone.

20　Terror overwhelms him, and he is blown away in the storms of the night.

21　The east wind carries him away, and he is gone. It sweeps him into eternity.

22　For God shall hurl at him unsparingly. He longs to flee from God.

23　Everyone will cheer at his death, and boo him into eternity.

CHAPTER 28

Men know how to mine silver and refine gold,
　　2　To dig iron from the earth and melt copper from stone.

3, 4 Men know how to put light into darkness so that a mine shaft can be sunk into the earth, and the earth searched and its deep secrets explored. Into the black rock, shadowed by death, men descend on ropes, swinging back and forth.

5 Men know how to obtain food from the surface of the earth, while underneath there is fire.

6 They know how to find sapphires and gold dust—

7 Treasures that no bird of prey can see, no eagle's eye observe—

8 For they are deep within the mines. No wild animal has ever walked upon those treasures; no lion has set his paw there.

9 Men know how to tear apart flinty rocks and how to overturn the roots of mountains.

10 They drill tunnels in the rocks and lay bare precious stones.

11 They dam up streams of water and pan the gold.[1]

12 But though men can do all these things, they don't know where to find wisdom and understanding.

13 They not only don't know how to get it, but, in fact, it is not to be found among the living.

14 'It's not here,' the oceans say; and the seas reply, 'Nor is it here.'

15 It cannot be bought for gold or silver,

16 Not for all the gold of Ophir or precious onyx stones or sapphires.

17 Wisdom is far more valuable than gold and

---

[1]Literally, "He brings forth to the light the things that are hidden."

glass. It cannot be bought for jewels mounted in fine gold.

18   Coral or crystal is worthless in trying to get it; its price is far above rubies.

19   Topaz from Ethiopia cannot purchase it, nor even the purest gold.

20   Then where can we get it? Where can it be found?

21   For it is hid from the eyes of all mankind; even the sharp-eyed birds in the sky cannot discover it.

22   But Destruction and Death speak of knowing something about it!

23, 24   And God surely knows where it is to be found, for He looks throughout the whole earth, under all the heavens.

25   He makes the winds blow and sets the boundaries of the oceans.

26   He makes the laws of the rain and a path for the lightning.

27   He knows where wisdom is and declares it to all who will listen. He established it and examined it thoroughly.

28   And this is what He says to all mankind: 'Look, to fear the Lord is true wisdom; to forsake evil is real understanding.' "

CHAPTER 29

Job continued:
        2   "Oh, for the years gone by when God took care of me,

3   When He lighted the way before me and I walked safely through the darkness;

4   Yes, in my early years, when the friendship of God was felt in my home;

5   When the Almighty was still with me and my children were around me;

6   When my projects prospered, and even the rock poured out streams of olive oil to me!

7   Those were the days when I went out to the city gate and took my place among the honored elders.

8   The young saw me and stepped aside, and even the aged rose and stood up in respect at my coming.

9   The princes stood in silence and laid their hands upon their mouths.

10   The highest officials of the city stood in quietness.

11   All rejoiced in what I said. All who saw me spoke well of me.

12   For I, as an honest judge,[1] helped the poor in their need, and the fatherless who had no one to help them.

13   I helped those who were ready to perish and they blessed me. And I caused the widows' hearts to sing for joy.

14   All I did was just and honest, for righteousness was my clothing!

15   I served as eyes for the blind and feet for the lame.

16   I was as a father to the poor, and saw to it that even strangers received a fair trial.

---

[1]Implied in verse 7.

17 I knocked out the fangs of the godless oppressors and made them drop their victims.

18 I thought, 'Surely I shall die quietly in my nest after a long, good life.'

19 For everything I did prospered; the dew lay all night upon my fields and watered them.

20 Fresh honors were constantly given me, and my abilities were constantly refreshed and renewed.

21 Everyone listened to me and valued my advice, and were silent until I spoke.

22 And after I spoke, they spoke no more, for my counsel satisfied them.

23 They longed for me to speak as those in drought-time long for rain. They waited eagerly with open mouths.

24 When they were discouraged, I smiled and that encouraged them, and lightened their spirits.

25 I told them what they should do, and corrected them as their chief, or as a king instructs his army, and as one who comforts those who mourn.

CHAPTER 30

But now those younger than I deride me—young men whose fathers are less than my dogs.

2 Oh, they have strong backs all right, but they are useless, stupid fools.

3 They are gaunt with famine and have been cast out into deserts and the wastelands, desolate and gloomy.

4 They eat roots and leaves,

5   Having been driven from civilization. Men shouted after them as after thieves.

6   So now they live in frightening ravines, and in caves, and among the rocks.

7   They sound like animals among the bushes, huddling together for shelter beneath the nettles.

8   These sons of theirs have also turned out to be fools, yes, children of no name, outcasts of civilization.

9   And now I have become the subject of their ribald song! I am a joke among *them!*

10   *They* despise me and won't come near me, and don't mind spitting in my face.

11   For God has placed my life in jeopardy. These young men, having humbled me, now cast off all restraint before me.

12   This rabble trip me and lay traps in my path.

13   They block my road and do everything they can to hasten my calamity, knowing full well that I have no one to help me.

14   They come at me from all directions. They rush upon me when I am down.

15   I live in terror now. They hold me in contempt and my prosperity has vanished as a cloud before a strong wind.

16   My heart is broken. Depression haunts my days.

17   My weary nights are filled with pain as though something were relentlessly gnawing at my bones.

18   All night long I toss and turn, and my garments bind about me.

19   God has thrown me into the mud. I have become as dust and ashes.

20   I cry to You, O God, but You don't answer me. I stand before You and You don't bother to look.

21   You have become cruel toward me, and persecute me with great power and effect.

22   You throw me into the whirlwind and dissolve me in the storm.

23   And I know that Your purpose for me is death.

24   I expected my fall to be broken, just as one who falls stretches out his hand or cries for help in his calamity.

25   And did I not weep for those in trouble? Wasn't I deeply grieved for the needy?

26   I therefore looked for good to come. Evil came instead. I waited for the light. Darkness came.

27   My heart is troubled and restless. Waves of affliction have come upon me.

28, 29   I am black, but not from sunburn. I stand up and cry to the assembly for help. [But I might as well save my breath,[1]] for I am considered a brother to jackals and a companion to ostriches.

30   My skin is black and peeling. My bones burn with fever.

31   The voice of joy and gladness has turned to mourning.

CHAPTER 31

I made a covenant with my eyes not to look with lust upon a girl.

---
[1]Implied.

2, 3   I know full well that Almighty God above sends calamity on those who do.

4   He sees everything I do, and every step I take.

5   If I have lied and deceived—

6   But God knows that I am innocent—

7, 8   Or if I have stepped off God's pathway, or if my heart has lusted for what my eyes have seen, or if I am guilty of any other sin, then let someone else reap the crops I have sown and let all that I have planted be rooted out.

9   Or if I have longed for another man's wife,

10   Then may I die, and may my wife be in another man's home, and someone else become her husband.

11   For lust is a shameful sin, a crime that should be punished.

12   It is a devastating fire that destroys to hell, and would root out all I have planted.

13   If I have been unfair to my servants,

14   How could I face God? What could I say when He questioned me about it?

15   For God made me, and made my servant too. He created us both.

16   If I have hurt the poor or caused widows to weep,

17   Or refused food to hungry orphans—

18   (But we have always cared for orphans in our home, treating them as our own children)—

19, 20   Or if I have seen anyone freezing and not given him clothing, or fleece from my sheep to keep him warm,

21 Or if I have taken advantage of an orphan because I thought I could get away with it—

22 If I have done any of these things, then let my arm be torn from its socket! Let my shoulder be wrenched out of place!

23 Rather that than face the judgment sent by God; that I dread more than anything else. For if the majesty of God opposes me, what hope is there?

24 If I have put my trust in money,

25 If my happiness depends on wealth,

26 Or if I have looked at the sun shining in the skies, or the moon walking down her silver pathway,

27 And my heart has been secretly enticed, and I have worshiped them by kissing my hand to them,

28 This, too, must be punished by the judges. For if I had done such things, it would mean that I denied the God of heaven.

29 If I have rejoiced at harm to an enemy—

30 (But actually I have never cursed anyone nor asked for revenge)—

31 Or if any of my servants have ever gone hungry—

32 (Actually I have never turned away even a stranger but have opened my doors to all)—

33 Or if, like Adam, I have tried to hide my sins,

34 Fearing the crowd and its contempt, so that I refused to acknowledge my sin and do not go out of my way to help others,—

35 (Oh, that there were someone who would listen to me and try to see my side of this argument. Look, I will sign my signature to my defense; now let the Al-

mighty show me that I am wrong; let *Him* approve the indictments made against me by my enemies.

36   I would treasure it like a crown.

37   Then I would tell Him exactly what I have done and why, presenting my defense as one He listens to)—

38, 39   Or if my land accuses me because I stole the fruit it bears, or if I have murdered its owners to get their land for myself,

40   Then let thistles grow on that land instead of wheat and weeds instead of barley."

Job's words are ended.

CHAPTER 32

The three men refused to reply further to Job because he kept insisting on his innocence.

2   Then Elihu (son of Barachel, the Buzite, of the Clan of Ram) became angry because Job refused to admit he had sinned and to acknowledge that God had just cause for punishing him.

3   But he was also angry with Job's three friends because they had been unable to answer Job's arguments and yet had condemned him.

4   Elihu had waited until now to speak because the others were older than he.

5   But when he saw that they had no further reply, he spoke out angrily,

6   And said, "I am young and you are old, so I held back and did not dare to tell you what I think,

7   For those who are older are said to be wiser;

8, 9   But it is not mere age that makes men wise.

Rather, it is the spirit in a man, the breath of the Almighty which makes him intelligent.

10   So listen to me awhile and let me express my opinion.

11, 12   I have waited all this time, listening very carefully to your arguments, but not one of them has convinced Job that he is a sinner, or has proved that he is.

13   And don't give me that line about 'only God can convince the sinner of his sin.'

14   If Job had been arguing with me, I would not answer with that kind of logic!

15   You sit there baffled, with no further replies.

16   Shall I then continue to wait when you are silent?

17   No, I will give my answer too.

18   For I am pent up and full of words, and the spirit within me urges me on.

19   I am like a wine cask without a vent! My words are ready to burst out!

20   I must speak to find relief, so let me give my answers.

21, 22   Don't insist that I be cautious lest I insult someone, and don't make me flatter anyone. Let me be frank, lest God should strike me dead.

CHAPTER 33

Please listen, Job, to what I have to say.

2   I have begun to speak; now let me continue.

3   I will speak the truth with all sincerity.

4   For the Spirit of God has made me, and the breath of the Almighty gives me life.

5   Don't hesitate to answer me if you can.

6   Look, I am the one you were wishing for, someone to stand between you and God and to be both His representative and yours.

7   You need not be frightened of me. I am not some person of renown to make you nervous and afraid. I, too, am made of common clay.

8   You have said it in my hearing, yes, you've said it again and again—

9   'I am pure, I am innocent; I have not sinned.'

10   You say God is using a fine-toothed comb to try to find a single fault, and so to count you as His enemy.

11   'And He puts my feet in the stocks,' you say, 'and watches every move I make.'

12   All right, here is my reply: In this very thing, you have sinned by speaking of God that way. For God is greater than man.

13   Why should you fight against Him just because He does not give account to you of what He does?

14   For God speaks again and again,

15   In dreams, in visions of the night when deep sleep falls on men as they lie on their beds.

16   He opens their ears in times like that, and gives them wisdom and instruction,

17, 18   Causing them to change their minds, and keeping them from pride, and warning them of the penalties of sin, and keeping them from falling into some trap.

19   Or, God sends sickness and pain, even though no bone is broken,

20   So that a man loses all taste and appetite for food and doesn't care for even the daintiest dessert.

21   He becomes thin, mere skin and bones,

22   And draws near to death.

23, 24   But if a messenger from heaven is there to intercede for him as a friend, to show him what is right, then God pities him and says,[1] 'Set him free. Do not make him die, for I have found a substitute.'

25   Then his body will become as healthy as a child's, firm and youthful again.

26   And when he prays to God, God will hear and answer and receive him with joy, and return him to his duties.

27   And he will declare to his friends, 'I sinned, but God let me go.

28   He did not let me die. I will go on living in the realm of light.'

29   Yes, God often does these things for man—

30   Brings back his soul from the pit, so that he may live in the light of the living.

31   Mark this well, O Job. Listen to me, and let me say more.

32   But if you have anything to say at this point, go ahead. I want to hear it, for I am anxious to justify you.

33   But if not, then listen to me. Keep silence and I will teach you wisdom!"

---

[1]Or, "and if the Angel says."

CHAPTER 34

E *lihu continued:*

2 "Listen to me, you wise men.

3 We can choose the sounds we want to listen to; we can choose the taste we want in food,

4 And we should choose to follow what is right. But first of all we must define among ourselves what is good.

5 For Job has said, 'I am innocent, but God says I'm not.

6 I am called a liar, even though I am innocent. I am horribly punished, even though I have not sinned.'

7, 8 Who else is as arrogant as Job? He must have spent much time with evil men,

9 For he said, 'Why waste time trying to please God?'

10 Listen to me, you with understanding. Surely everyone knows that *God doesn't sin!*

11 Rather, He punishes the sinners.

12 There is no truer statement than this: *God is never wicked or unjust.*

13 He alone has authority over the earth and dispenses justice for the world.

14 If God were to withdraw His Spirit,

15 All life would disappear and mankind would turn again to dust.

16 Listen now and try to understand.

17 Could God govern if He hated justice? Are you going to condemn the Almighty Judge?

18   Are you going to condemn this God who says to kings and nobles, 'You are wicked and unjust'?

19   For He doesn't care how great a man may be, and doesn't pay any more attention to the rich than to the poor. He made them all.

20   In a moment they die, and at midnight great and small shall suddenly pass away, removed by no human hand.

21   For God carefully watches the goings on of all mankind; He sees them all.

22   No darkness is thick enough to hide evil men from His eyes;

23   So there is no need to wait for some great crime before a man is called before God in judgment.

24   Without making a federal case of it, God simply shatters the greatest of men, and puts others in their place.

25   He watches what they do and in a single night He overturns them, destroying them,

26   Or openly strikes them down as wicked men.

27   For they turned aside from following Him,

28   Causing the cry of the poor to come to the attention of God. Yes, He hears the cries of those being oppressed.

29, 30   Yet when He chooses not to speak, who can criticize? Again, He may prevent a vile man from ruling, thus saving a nation from ruin, and He can depose an entire nation just as easily.

31   Why don't people exclaim to their God, 'We have sinned, but we will stop'?

32   Or, 'We know not what evil we have done; only tell us, and we will cease at once.'

33   Must God tailor His justice to your demands? Must He change the order of the universe to suit your whims? The answer must be obvious even to you!

34, 35   Anyone even half-bright will agree with me that you, Job, are speaking like a fool.

36   You should be given the maximum penalty for the wicked way you have talked about God.

37   For now you have added rebellion, arrogance and blasphemy to your other sins."

CHAPTER 35

E *lihu continued:*
2, 3   "Do you think it is right for you to claim, 'I haven't sinned, but I'm no better off before God than if I had'?

4   I will answer you, and all your friends too.

5   Look up there into the sky, high above you.

6   If you sin, does that shake the heavens and knock God from His throne? Even if you sin again and again, what effect will it have upon Him?

7   Or if you are good, is this some great gift to Him?

8   Your sins may hurt another man, or your good deeds may profit him.

9, 10   The oppressed may shriek beneath their wrongs and groan beneath the power of the rich; yet none of them cry to God, asking 'Where is God my Maker who gives songs in the night,

11   And makes us a little wiser than the animals and birds?'

12   But when anyone does cry out this question to Him, He never replies by instant punishment of the tyrants.[1]

13   But it is false to say He doesn't hear those cries;

14, 15   And it is even more false to say that He doesn't see what is going on. He *does* bring about justice at last, if you will only wait. But do you cry out against Him because He does not instantly respond in anger?

16   Job, you have spoken like a fool."

CHAPTER 36

Elihu continued:

2   "Let me go on and I will show you the truth of what I am saying. For I have not finished defending God!

3   I will give you many illustrations of the righteousness of my Maker.

4   I am telling you the honest truth, for I am a man of well-rounded knowledge.

5   God is almighty and yet does not despise anyone! And He is perfect in His understanding.

6   He does not reward the wicked with His blessings, but gives them their full share of punishment.

7   He does not ignore the good men but honors them by placing them upon eternal, kingly thrones.

8   If troubles come upon them, and they are enslaved and afflicted,

---

[1]Or, "because of man's base pride."

9 Then He takes the trouble to point out to them the reason, what they have done that is wrong, or how they have behaved proudly.

10 He helps them hear His instruction to turn away from their sin.

11 If they listen and obey Him, then they will be blessed with prosperity throughout their lives.

12 If they won't listen to Him, they shall perish in battle and die because of their lack of good sense.

13 But the godless reap His anger. They do not even return to Him when He punishes them.

14 They die young after lives of dissipation and depravity.

15 He delivers by distress! This makes them listen to Him!

16 How He wanted to lure you away from danger into a wide and pleasant valley and to prosper you there.

17 But you are too preoccupied with your imagined grievances against others.

18 Watch out! Don't let your anger at others lead you into scoffing at God! Don't let your suffering embitter you at the only one who can deliver you.

19 Do you really think that if you shout loudly enough against God, He will be ashamed and repent? Will this put an end to your chastisement?

20 Do not desire the nighttime, with its opportunities for crime.

21 Turn back from evil, for it was to prevent you from getting into a life of evil that God sent this suffering.

22 Look, God is all-powerful. Who is a teacher like Him?

23 Who can say that what He does is absurd or evil?

24 Instead, glorify Him for His mighty works for which He is so famous.

25 Everyone has seen these things from a distance.

26 God is so great that we cannot begin to know Him. No one can begin to understand eternity.

27 He draws up the water vapor and then distills it into rain,

28 Which the skies pour down.

29 Can anyone really understand the spreading of the clouds, and the thunders within?

30 See how He spreads the lightning around Him, and blankets the tops of the mountains.

31 By His fantastic powers in nature He punishes or blesses the people, giving them food in abundance.

32 He fills His hands with lightning bolts. He hurls each at its target.

33 We feel His presence in the thunder. May all sinners be warned.[1]

CHAPTER 37

My heart trembles at this.
2 Listen, listen to the thunder of His voice.

3 It rolls across the heavens and His lightning flashes out in every direction.

---

[1]Literally, "(even) the cattle (warn us) of the coming storm."

4   Afterwards comes the roaring of the thunder—the tremendous voice of His majesty.

5   His voice is glorious in the thunder. We cannot comprehend the greatness of His power.

6   For He directs the snow, the showers, and storm to fall upon the earth.

7   Man's work stops at such a time, so that all men everywhere may recognize His power.

8   The wild animals hide in the rocks or in their dens.

9   From the south comes the rain; from the north, the cold.

10   God blows upon the rivers, and even the widest torrents freeze.

11   He loads the clouds with moisture and they send forth His lightning.

12   The lightning bolts are directed by His hand, and do whatever He commands throughout the earth.

13   He sends the storms[1] as punishment, or, in His loving-kindness, to encourage.

14   Listen, O Job, stop and consider the wonderful miracles of God.

15   Do you know how God controls all nature, and causes the lightning to flash forth from the clouds?

16, 17   Do you understand the balancing of the clouds with wonderful perfection and skill? Do you know why you become warm when the south wind is blowing and everything is still?

18   Can you spread out the gigantic mirror of the skies as He does?

---

[1]Implied.

19, 20 You who think you know so much,[2] teach the rest of us how we should approach God. For we are too dull to know! With your wisdom, would we then dare to approach Him? Well, does a man wish to be swallowed alive?

21 For as we cannot look at the sun for its brightness when the winds have cleared away the clouds,

22 Neither can we gaze at the terrible majesty of God breaking forth upon us from Heaven, clothed in dazzling splendor.

23 We cannot imagine the power of the Almighty, and yet He is so just and merciful that He does not destroy us.

24 No wonder men everywhere fear Him! For He is not impressed by the world's wisest men!"

CHAPTER 38

Then the Lord answered Job from the whirlwind:

2 "Why are you using your ignorance to deny My providence?

3 Now get ready to fight, for I am going to demand some answers from you, and you must reply.

4 Where were you when I laid the foundations of the earth? Tell me, if you know so much.

5 Do you know how its dimensions were determined, and who did the surveying?

6, 7 What supports its foundations, and who laid its cornerstone, as the morning stars sang together and all the angels shouted for joy?

---

[2]Implied.

8, 9　Who decreed the boundaries of the seas when they gushed from the depths? Who clothed them with clouds and thick darkness,

10　And barred them by limiting their shores?

11　And said, 'Thus far and no farther shall you come, and here shall your proud waves stop!'?

12　Have you ever once commanded the morning to appear, and caused the dawn to rise in the east?

13　Have you ever told the daylight to spread to the ends of the earth, to end the night's wickedness?

14　Have you ever robed the dawn in red,

15　And disturbed the haunts of wicked men and stopped the arm raised to strike?

16　Have you explored the springs from which the seas come, or walked in the sources of their depths?

17, 18　Has the location of the gates of Death been revealed to you? Do you realize the extent of the earth? Tell Me about it if you know!

19　Where does the light come from, and how do you get there? Or tell Me about the darkness. Where does it come from?

20　Can you find its boundaries, or go to its source?

21　But of course you know all this! For you were born before it was all created, and you are so very experienced!

22, 23　Have you visited the treasuries of the snow, or seen where hail is made and stored? For I have reserved it for the time when I will need it in war.

24　Where is the path to the distribution point of light? Where is the home of the east wind?

25-27　Who dug the valleys for the torrents of rain?

Who laid out the path for the lightning, causing the rain to fall upon the barren deserts, so that the parched and barren ground is satisfied with water, and tender grass springs up?

28   Has the rain a father? Where does dew come from?

29   Whose mother is the ice and frost?

30   For the water changes and turns to ice, as hard as rock.

31   Can you hold back the stars? Can you restrain Orion or Pleiades?

32   Can you ensure the proper sequence of the seasons, or guide the constellation of the Bear with her satellites across the heavens?

33   Do you know the laws of the universe and how the heavens influence the earth?

34   Can you shout to the clouds and make it rain?

35   Can you make lightning appear and cause it to strike as you direct it?

36   Who gives intuition and instinct?[1]

37, 38   Who is wise enough to number all the clouds? Who can tilt the water jars of heaven, when everything is dust and clods?

39, 40   Can you stalk prey like a lioness, to satisfy the young lions' appetites as they lie in their dens, or lie in wait in the jungle?

41   Who provides for the ravens when their young cry out to God as they try to struggle up from their nest in hunger?

---

[1]Or, "Who has put wisdom in the inward parts, and given understanding to the mind?"

CHAPTER 39

Do you know how mountain goats give birth? Have you ever seen them giving birth to their young?

2, 3   Do you know how many months of pregnancy they have before they bow themselves to give birth to their young, and carry their burden no longer?

4   Their young grow up in the open field, then leave their parents and return to them no more.

5   Who makes the wild donkeys wild?

6   I have placed them in the wilderness and given them salt plains to live in.

7   For they hate the noise of the city and want no drivers shouting at them!

8   The mountain ranges are their pastureland; there they search for every blade of grass.

9   Will the wild ox be your happy servant? Will he stay beside your feeding crib?

10   Can you use a wild ox to plow with? Will he pull the harrow for you?

11   Because he is so strong, will you trust him? Will you let him decide where to work?

12   Can you send him out to bring in the grain from the threshing-floor?

13   The ostrich flaps her wings grandly, but has no true motherly love.

14   She lays her eggs on top of the earth, to warm them in the dust.

15   She forgets that someone may step on them and crush them, or the wild animals destroy them.

16　She ignores her young as though they weren't her own, and is unconcerned though they die.

17　For God has deprived her of wisdom.

18　But whenever she jumps up to run, she passes the swiftest horse with its rider.

19　Have you given the horse strength, or clothed his neck with a quivering mane?

20　Have you made him able to leap forward like a locust? His majestic snorting is something to hear!

21-23　He paws the earth and rejoices in his strength, and when he goes to war, he is unafraid and does not run away though the arrows rattle against him, or the flashing spear and javelin.

24　Fiercely he paws the ground and rushes forward into battle when the trumpet blows.

25　At the sound of the bugle he shouts, 'Aha!' He smells the battle when far away. He rejoices at the shouts of battle and the roar of the captain's commands.

26　Do you know how a hawk soars and spreads her wings to the south?

27　Is it at your command that the eagle rises high upon the cliffs to make her nest?

28　She lives upon the cliffs, making her home in her mountain fortress.

29　From there she spies her prey, from a very great distance.

30　Her nestlings gulp down blood, for she goes wherever the slain are."

Chapter 40

The Lord went on:

2   "Do you still want to argue with the Almighty? Or will you yield? Do you—God's critic—have the answers?"

3   *Then Job replied to God:*

4   "I am nothing—how could I ever find the answers? I lay my hand upon my mouth in silence.

5   I have said too much already."

6   *Then the Lord spoke to Job again from the whirlwind:*

7   "Stand up like a man and brace yourself for battle. Let Me ask you a question, and give Me the answer.

8   Are you going to discredit My justice and condemn Me, so that you can say you are right?

9   Are you as strong as God, and can you shout as loudly as He?

10   All right then, put on your robes of state, your majesty and splendor.

11   Give vent to your anger. Let it overflow against the proud.

12   Humiliate the haughty with a glance; tread down the wicked where they stand.

13   Knock them into the dust, stone-faced in death.

14   If you can do that, then I'll agree with you that your own strength can save you.

15   Take a look at the behemoth! I made him, too, just as I made you! He eats grass like an ox.

16 See his powerful loins and the muscles of his belly.

17 His tail is as straight as a cedar. The sinews of his thighs are tightly knit together.

18 His vertebrae lie straight as a tube of brass. His ribs are like iron bars.

19 How ferocious he is among all of God's creation, so let whoever hopes to master him bring a sharp sword!

20 The mountains offer their best food to him—the other wild animals on which he preys.

21 He lies down under the lotus plants, hidden by the reeds,

22 Covered by their shade among the willows there beside the stream.

23 He is not disturbed by raging rivers, not even when the swelling Jordan rushes down upon him.

24 No one can catch him off guard or put a ring in his nose and lead him away.

CHAPTER 41

Can you catch leviathan with a hook and line? Or put a noose around his tongue?

2 Can you tie him with a rope through the nose, or pierce his jaw with a spike?

3 Will he beg you to desist or try to flatter you from your intentions?

4 Will he agree to let you make him your slave for life?

5 Can you make a pet of him like a bird, or give him to your little girls to play with?

6 Do fishing partners sell him to the fish-mongers?

7 Will his hide be hurt by darts, or his head with a harpoon?

8 If you lay your hands upon him, you will long remember the battle that ensues, and you will never try it again!

9 No, it's useless to try to capture him. It is frightening even to think about it!

10 No one dares to stir *him* up, let alone try to conquer him. And if no one can stand before *him,* who can stand before *Me?*

11 I owe no one anything. Everything under the heaven is Mine.

12 I should mention, too, the tremendous strength in his limbs, and throughout his enormous frame.

13 Who can penetrate his hide, or who dares come within reach of his jaws?

14 For his teeth are terrible.

15-17 His overlapping scales are his pride, making a tight seal, so no air can get between them, and nothing can penetrate.

18 When he sneezes, the sunlight sparkles like lightning across the vapor droplets. His eyes glow like sparks.

19 Fire leaps from his mouth.

20 Smoke flows from his nostrils, like steam from a boiling pot that is fired by dry rushes.

21 Yes, his breath would kindle coals—flames leap from his mouth.

22 The tremendous strength in his neck strikes terror wherever he goes.

23   His flesh is hard and firm, not soft and fat.

24   His heart is hard as rock, just like a millstone.

25   When he stands up, the strongest are afraid. Terror grips them.

26   No sword can stop him, nor spear nor dart nor pointed shaft.

27, 28   Iron is nothing but straw to him, and brass is rotten wood. Arrows cannot make him flee. Slingstones are as ineffective as straw.

29   Clubs do no good, and he laughs at the javelins hurled at him.

30   His belly is covered with scales as sharp as shards; he drags across the ground like a steamroller!

31, 32   He makes the water boil with his commotion. He churns the depths. He leaves a shining wake of froth behind him. One would think the sea was made of frost!

33   There is nothing else so fearless anywhere on earth.

34   Of all the beasts, he is the proudest—monarch of all that he sees."

CHAPTER 42

Then Job replied to God:

2   "I know that You can do anything and that no one can stop You.

3   You ask who it is who has so foolishly denied Your providence. It is I. I was talking about things I knew nothing about and did not understand, things far too wonderful for me.

4 [You said,[1]] 'Listen and I will speak! Let me put the question to you! See if you can answer them!'

5 [But now I say,[1]] 'I had heard about You before, but now I have seen You,

6 And I loathe myself and repent in dust and ashes.' "

7 *After the Lord had finished speaking with Job, He said to Eliphaz the Temanite:* "I am angry with you and with your two friends, for you have not been right in what you have said about Me, as My servant Job was.

8 Now take seven young bulls and seven rams and go to my servant Job and offer a burnt offering for yourselves; and my servant Job will pray for you, and I will accept his prayer on your behalf, and won't destroy you as I should because of your sin, your failure to speak rightly concerning my servant Job."

9 So Eliphaz the Temanite, and Bildad the Shuhite, and Zophar the Naamathite did as the Lord commanded them, and the Lord accepted Job's prayer on their behalf.

10 Then, when Job prayed for his friends, the Lord restored his wealth and happiness! In fact, the Lord gave him twice as much as before!

11 Then all of his brothers, sisters, and former friends arrived and feasted with him in his home, consoling him for all his sorrow, and comforting him because of all the trials the Lord had brought upon him. And each of them brought him a gift of money, and a gold ring.

---

[1]Implied.

12 So the Lord blessed Job at the end of his life more than at the beginning. For now he had 14,000 sheep, 6,000 camels, 1,000 teams of oxen, and 1,000 female donkeys.

13 God also gave him seven more sons and three more daughters.[2]

14 These were the names of his daughters:
Jemima
Kezia
Keren,[3]

15 And in all the land there were no other girls as lovely as the daughters of Job; and their father put them into his will along with their brothers.

16 Job lived 140 years after that, living to see his grandchildren and great-grandchildren too.

17 Then at last he died, an old, old man, after living a long, good life.

---

[2]Making a total of 20 children, twice as many as he had before. (Ten were in heaven.)
[3]Literally, "Keren-Happuch."

The Song of Solomon

CHAPTER 1

This song of songs, more wonderful than any other, was composed by King Solomon:

The Girl:[1]

2 "Kiss me again and again, for your love is sweeter than wine!

3 How fragrant your cologne, and how great your name! No wonder all the young girls love you!

4 Take me with you; come, let's run!"

*   *   *   *   *

The Girl:

"The king has brought me into his palace! How happy we will be! Your love is better than wine! No wonder all the young girls love you!"

*   *   *   *   *

The Girl:

5 "I am dark but beautiful, O girls of Jerusalem, tanned as the dark tents of Kedar."

*   *   *   *   *

King Solomon:

"But lovely as the silken tents of Solomon!"

---

[1]The headings identifying the speakers are conjectures and are not in the original text.

The Girl:

6　"Don't look down on me, you city girls,[2] just because my complexion is so dark—the sun has tanned me. My brothers were angry with me and sent me out into the sun[3] to tend the vineyards, but see what it has done to me![4]"

*　　*　　*　　*　　*

The Girl:

7　"Tell me, O one I love, where are you leading your flock today? Where will you be at noon? For I will come and join you there instead of wandering like a vagabond among the flocks of your companions."

*　　*　　*　　*　　*

King Solomon:

8　"If you don't know, O most beautiful woman in all the world, follow the trail of my flock to the shepherds' tents, and there feed your sheep and their lambs.

9　What a lovely filly[5] you are, my love!

10　How lovely your cheeks are, with your hair[6] falling down upon them! How stately your neck with that long string of jewels.

11　We shall make you golden earrings and silver beads."

*　　*　　*　　*　　*

The Girl:

12　"The king lies on his bed, enchanted by the fragrance of my perfume.

---

[2]Implied in verse 5.
[3]Implied.
[4]Literally, "but my own vineyards are neglected."
[5]Literally, "I compare you to my mare harnessed to Pharaoh's chariot."
[6]Literally, "ornaments."

13   My beloved one is a sachet of myrrh lying between my breasts."

*   *   *   *   *

King Solomon:

14   "My beloved is a bouquet of flowers in the
gardens of Engedi.

15   How beautiful you are, my love, how beautiful!
Your eyes are soft as doves'.

16   What a lovely, pleasant thing you are, lying here
upon the grass,

17   Shaded by the cedar trees and firs."

CHAPTER 2

The Girl:
        "I am the rose of Sharon, the lily of the valley."

*   *   *   *   *

King Solomon:

2   "Yes, a lily among thorns, so is my beloved as
compared with any other girls."

*   *   *   *   *

The Girl:

3   "My lover is an apple tree, the finest in the
orchard as compared with any of the other youths. I am
seated in his much-desired shade and his fruit is lovely
to eat.

4   He brings me to the banquet hall and everyone
can see how much he loves me.

5   Oh, feed me with your love—your 'raisins' and
your 'apples'—for I am utterly lovesick!

6   His left hand is under my head and with his right hand he embraces me.

7   O girls of Jerusalem, I adjure you by the gazelles and deer in the park, that you do not awaken my lover. Let him sleep![1]"

*   *   *   *   *

The Girl:

8   "Ah, I hear him—my beloved! Here he comes, leaping upon the mountains and bounding over the hills.

9   My beloved is like a gazelle or young deer. Look, there he is behind the wall, now looking in at the windows!

10   My beloved said to me, 'Rise up, my love, my fair one, and come away.

11   For the winter is past, the rain is over and gone.

12   The flowers are springing up and the time of the singing of birds has come. Yes, spring is here.[2]

13   The leaves are coming out[3] and the grape vines are in blossom. How delicious they smell! Arise, my love, my fair one, and come away.'

14   My dove is hiding behind some rocks, behind an outcrop of the cliff. Call to me and let me hear your lovely voice and see your handsome face.

*   *   *   *   *

15   The little foxes are ruining the vineyards. Catch them, for the grapes are all in blossom.

*   *   *   *   *

---

[1]Literally, "that you stir not up nor awaken love until it please."
[2]Literally, "The voice of the turtledove is heard in our land."
[3]Literally, "The fig tree puts forth its figs."

16   My beloved is mine and I am his. He is feeding among the lilies!

17   Before the dawn comes and the shadows flee away, come to me, my beloved, and be like a gazelle or a young stag on the mountains of spices."

CHAPTER 3

The Girl:
   "One night my lover was missing from my bed. I got up to look for him but couldn't find him.

2   I went out into the streets of the city and the roads to seek him, but I searched in vain.

3   The police stopped me and I said to them, 'Have you seen him anywhere, this one I love so much?'

4   It was only a little while afterwards that I found him and held him and would not let him go until I had brought him into my childhood home, into my mother's old bedroom.

5   I adjure you, O women of Jerusalem, by the gazelles and deer of the park, not to awake my lover. Let him sleep."

*   *   *   *   *

The Young Women of Jerusalem:
6   "Who is this sweeping in from the deserts like a cloud of smoke along the ground, smelling of myrrh and frankincense and every other spice that can be bought?

7   Look, it is the chariot[1] of Solomon with sixty of the mightiest men of his army surrounding it.

---
[1]Literally, "litter."

8   They are all skilled swordsmen and experienced bodyguards. Each one has his sword upon his thigh to defend their king against any onslaught in the night.

9   For King Solomon made himself a chariot from the wood of Lebanon.

10   Its posts are silver, its canopy gold, the seat is purple; and the back is inlaid with these words: 'With love from the girls of Jerusalem!' "

The Girl:

11   "Go out and see King Solomon, O young women of Zion; see the crown with which his mother crowned him on his wedding day, his day of gladness."

CHAPTER 4

King Solomon:

"How beautiful you are, my love, how beautiful! Your eyes are those of doves. Your hair falls across your face like flocks of goats that frisk across the slopes of Gilead!

2   Your teeth are white as sheep's wool, newly shorn and washed; perfectly matched, without one missing.

3   Your lips are like a thread of scarlet—and how beautiful your mouth. Your cheeks are matched love-liness[1] behind your locks.[2]

4   Your neck is stately[3] as the tower of David, jeweled with a thousand heroes' shields.

5   Your breasts are like twin fawns of a gazelle, feeding among the lilies.

---

[1]Literally. "like halves of a pomegranate."
[2]Literally, "behind your veil."
[3]Implied.

6   Until the morning dawns and the shadows flee away, I will go to the mountain of myrrh and to the hill of frankincense.

7   You are so beautiful, my love, in every part of you.

8   Come with me from Lebanon, my bride. We will look down from the summit of the mountain, from the top of Mount Hermon,[4] where the lions have their dens, and panthers prowl.

9   You have ravished my heart, my lovely one, my bride; I am overcome by one glance of your eyes, by a single bead of your necklace.

10   How sweet is your love, my darling, my bride. How much better it is than mere wine. The perfume of your love is more fragrant than all the richest spices.

11   Your lips, my dear, are made of honey. Yes, honey and cream are under your tongue, and the scent of your garments is like the scent of the mountains and cedars of Lebanon.

12   My darling bride is like a private garden, a spring that no one else can have, a fountain of my own.

13, 14   You are like a lovely orchard bearing precious fruit,[5] with the rarest of perfumes; nard and saffron, calamus and cinnamon, and perfume from every other incense tree; as well as myrrh and aloes, and every other lovely spice.

15   You are a garden fountain, a well of living water, refreshing as the streams from the Lebanon mountains."

*   *   *   *   *

---

[4]Literally, "Depart from the peak of Amana, from the peak of Senir and Hermon."
[5]Literally, "Your shoots are an orchard of pomegranates . . ."

The Girl:

16 "Come, north wind, awaken; come, south wind, blow upon my garden and waft its lovely perfume to my beloved. Let him come into his garden and eat its choicest fruits."

CHAPTER 5

King Solomon:
"I am here in my garden, my darling, my bride! I gather my myrrh with my spices and eat my honeycomb with my honey. I drink my wine with my milk."

*　　*　　*　　*　　*

The Young Women of Jerusalem:

"Oh, lover and beloved, eat and drink! Yes, drink deeply!"

*　　*　　*　　*　　*

The Girl:

2 "One night as I was sleeping, my heart awakened in a dream. I heard the voice of my beloved; he was knocking at my bedroom door. 'Open to me, my darling, my lover, my lovely dove,' he said, 'for I have been out in the night and am covered with dew.'

3 But I said, 'I have disrobed. Shall I get dressed again? I have washed my feet, and should I get them soiled?'

4 My beloved tried to unlatch the door and my heart was moved for him.

5 I jumped up to open it and my hands dripped with perfume, my fingers with lovely myrrh as I pulled back the bolt.

6 I opened to my beloved, but he was gone. My heart stopped. I searched for him but couldn't find him anywhere. I called to him, but there was no reply.

7 The guards found me and struck and wounded me. The watchman on the wall tore off my veil.

8 I adjure you, O women of Jerusalem, if you find my beloved one, tell him that I am sick with love."

* * * * *

The Young Women of Jerusalem:

9 "O woman of rare beauty, what is it about your loved one that is better than any other, that you command us this?"

* * * * *

The Girl:

10 "My beloved one is tanned and handsome, better than ten thousand others!

11 His head is purest gold! And he has wavy, raven hair.

12 His eyes are like doves beside the water brooks, deep and quiet.

13 His cheeks are like sweetly scented beds of spices. His lips are perfumed lilies, his breath like myrrh.

14 His arms are round bars of gold set with topaz; his body is bright ivory encrusted with jewels.

15 His legs are as pillars of marble set in sockets of finest gold, like cedars of Lebanon; none can rival him.

16 His mouth is altogether sweet, lovable in every way. Such, O women of Jerusalem, is my beloved, my friend."

CHAPTER 6

The Young Women of Jerusalem:

"O rarest of beautiful women, where has your loved one gone? We will help you find him."

*　　*　　*　　*　　*

The Girl:

2　"He has gone down to his garden, to his spice beds, to pasture his flock and to gather the lilies.

3　I am my beloved's and my beloved is mine. He pastures his flock among the lilies!"

*　　*　　*　　*　　*

King Solomon:

4　"O my beloved, you are as beautiful as the lovely land of Tirzah, yes, beautiful as Jerusalem, and how you capture my heart.[1]

5　Look the other way, for your eyes have overcome me! Your hair, as it falls across your face, is like a flock of goats frisking down the slopes of Gilead.

6　Your teeth are white as freshly washed ewes, perfectly matched and not one missing.

7　Your cheeks are matched loveliness[2] behind your hair.

8　I have sixty other wives, all queens, and eighty concubines, and unnumbered virgins available to me:

9　But you, my dove, my perfect one, are the only one among them all, without an equal! The women of

---

[1] Literally, "You are . . . terrible as an army with banners."
[2] Literally, "like the halves of a pomegranate."

Jerusalem were delighted when they saw you and even the queens and concubines praise you.

10   'Who is this,' they ask, 'arising as the dawn, fair as the moon, pure as the sun, so utterly captivating?[3]' "

*   *   *   *   *

The Girl:

11   "I went down into the orchard of nuts and out to the valley to see the springtime there, to see whether the grapevines were budding or the pomegranates were blossoming yet.

12   Before I realized it I was stricken with terrible homesickness and wanted to be back among my own people.[4]"

*   *   *   *   *

The Young Women of Jerusalem:

13   "Return, return to us, O maid of Shulam. Come back, come back, that we may see you once again."

*   *   *   *   *

The Girl:
"Why should you seek a mere Shulammite?"
King Solomon:
"Because you dance so beautifully.[5]"

CHAPTER 7

King Solomon:
    "How beautiful your tripping feet, O queenly maiden. Your rounded thighs are like jewels, the work of the most skilled of craftsmen.

---

[3]Literally, "terrible as an army with banners."
[4]Literally, "the chariots of my princely people." Another possible reading is, "terrible desire to sit beside my beloved in his chariot."
[5]Literally, "as upon a dance before two armies."

2 Your navel is lovely as a goblet filled with wine. Your waist[1] is like a heap of wheat set about with lilies.

3 Your two breasts are like two fawns, yes, lovely twins.[2]

4 Your neck is stately as an ivory tower, your eyes as limpid pools in Heshbon by the gate of Bath-rabbim. Your nose is shapely[3] like the tower of Lebanon over-looking Damascus.

5 As Mount Carmel crowns the mountains, so your hair is your crown. The king is held captive in your queenly tresses.

6 Oh, how delightful you are; how pleasant, O love, for utter delight!

7 You are tall and slim like a palm tree, and your breasts are like its clusters of dates.

8 I said, I will climb up into the palm tree and take hold of its branches. Now may your breasts be like grape clusters, and the scent of your breath like apples,

9 And your kisses as exciting as the best of wine, smooth and sweet, causing the lips of those who are asleep to speak."

*   *   *   *   *

The Girl:

10 "I am my beloved's and I am the one he desires.

11 Come, my beloved, let us go out into the fields and stay in the villages.

12 Let us get up early and go out to the vineyards

---

[1]Literally, "belly."
[2]Literally, "twins of a gazelle."
[3]Implied.

and see whether the vines have budded and whether the blossoms have opened and whether the pomegranates are in flower. And there I will give you my love.

13 There the mandrakes give forth their fragrance and the rarest fruits are at our doors, the new as well as old, for I have stored them up for my beloved."

CHAPTER 8

The Girl:

"Oh, if only you were my brother; then I could kiss you no matter who was watching, and no one would laugh at me!

2 I would bring you to my childhood home,[1] and there you would teach me. I would give you spiced wine to drink, sweet pomegranate wine.

3 His left hand would be under my head and his right hand would embrace me.

4 I adjure you, O women of Jerusalem, not to awaken him until he please."

* * * * *

The Young Women of Jerusalem:

5 "Who is this coming up from the desert, leaning on her beloved?"

* * * * *

King Solomon:

"Under the apple tree where your mother gave birth to you in her travail, there I awakened your love."

* * * * *

---

[1]Literally, "my mother's house."

The Girl:

6   "Seal me in your heart with permanent betrothal, for love is strong as death and jealousy is as cruel as Sheol. It flashes fire, the very flame of Jehovah.

7   Many waters cannot quench the flame of love, neither can the floods drown it. If a man tried to buy it with everything he owned, he couldn't do it."

*   *   *   *   *

The Girl:

8   "We have a little sister too young for breasts. What shall we do if someone asks to marry her?"

*   *   *   *   *

King Solomon:

9   "If she has no breasts[2] we will build upon her a battlement of silver,[3] and if she is a door we will enclose her with cedar boards![3]"

*   *   *   *   *

The Girl:

10   "I am slim, tall,[4] and full-breasted[5] and I have found favor in my lover's eyes.

11   Solomon had a vineyard at Baal-hamon which he rented out to some farmers there, the rent being one thousand pieces of silver from each.

12   But as for my own vineyard, you, O Solomon,

---

[2] Literally, "if she be a wall."
[3] The meaning is obscure.
[4] Literally, "I am as a wall."
[5] Literally, "My breasts are its towers."

shall have my thousand pieces of silver and I will give two hundred pieces to those who care for it.

13 O my beloved, living in the gardens, how wonderful that your companions may listen to your voice; let me hear it too.

14 Come quickly, my beloved, and be like a gazelle or young deer upon the mountains of spices."